Cognition

Second Edition

D0224562

TEST-ITEM FILE

Cognition

SECOND EDITION

Cara Laney
REED COLLEGE

Friderike Heuer
LEWIS & CLARK COLLEGE

 W • W • NORTON & COMPANY • NEW YORK • LONDON

Copyright © 2001 by W. W. Norton & Company, Inc.

All rights reserved

Printed in the United States of America

ISBN 0-393-97716-1 (pbk.)

W. W. Norton & Company, Inc., 500 Fifth Avenue, New York, NY 10110
www.wwnorton.com

W. W. Norton & Company Ltd., Castle House, 75/76 Wells Street, London W1T 3QT

1 2 3 4 5 6 7 8 9 0

CONTENTS

PREFACE

To the instructor

The test items for each chapter are designed to include a mix of questions: questions probing students' understanding of basic terms and simple facts and questions probing students' broader comprehension of the issues covered in the text chapters. This set of multiple (and often competing) goals has led to some overlap among the questions within each chapter's set. It is my assumption that any instructor is likely to use only a subset of the questions for each chapter. Enough questions have been proposed so that most instructors will find an appropriately sized set of questions for each chapter.

If you, the instructor, discover any problems in the questions (e.g., miskeyed or ambiguous items), I would appreciate hearing about them. Likewise, comments about the question set for each chapter (e.g., coverage or level of difficulty) would also be welcome. Feedback can be either sent to me, care of W. W. Norton, or e-mailed to this address: cogtext@reed.edu.

CHAPTER 1 | The Science of the Mind

1. Which of the following is likely to be stored in episodic memory?
   a. your recollection of what you had to eat last New Year's Eve
   b. your knowing that the word "table" names a type of furniture
   c. your recall of what the color red looks like
   d. your knowledge that people tend to be happy when they receive gifts.

   Answer: a

2. Which of the following is likely not to be based on knowledge stored in generic memory?
   a. you know that a child's piggy bank is likely to contain coins, not paper money.
   b. you recall when you learned that your friend Susan is a vegetarian.
   c. you know the name of the first U.S. president.
   d. if you want to write a note, you know that a pen or pencil will be useful.

   Answer: b

3. You easily remember the opposite of "hot." This is an example of:
   a. generic memory.
   b. episodic memory.
   c. implicit memory.
   d. sensory memory.

   Answer: a

4. When you understand a simple children's story, you rely on generic memory for all of the following *except*:
   a. recalling the meaning of the individual words within the story.
   b. supplying background knowledge needed to fill in gaps in the story.

    c. providing knowledge that guides your interpretation of unclear aspects of the story.

    d. recalling when you heard the same story before.

Answer: d

5. Patients suffering from clinical amnesia are characterized by a disorder in their:
   a. memory.
   b. ability to recognize patterns.
   c. speech.
   d. ability to comprehend language.

Answer: a

6. Which of the following descriptive statements is *least likely* to appear in a description of an amnesia patient, such as H.M.?
   a. "He can not remember what he did earlier today—including events that took place just an hour ago."
   b. "He read this story last month, but he was still surprised by how the story turned out."
   c. "Even though he has encountered the nurse many times, he is still unable to recognize her."
   d. "He has gradually adjusted over the last few months to the news of his uncle's death."

Answer: d

7. The term "introspection" refers to:
   a. the process through which one individual seeks to infer the thoughts of another individual.
   b. the procedure of examining thought processing by monitoring the brain's electrical activity.
   c. the process of each person looking within, to observe his or her own thoughts and ideas.
   d. the technique of studying thought by interpreting the symbols used in communication.

Answer: c

8. A participant is asked to look within him/herself and report on his/her own mental processes. This method is called:
   a. self-reflection.
   b. self-monitoring.
   c. introspection.
   d. mentalistic study.

Answer: c

9. Which of the following is *not* a concern about the use of introspection as a research tool?
   a. a verbal report based on introspection may provide a distorted picture of mental processes that were nonverbal in nature.
   b. different participants use different terms to describe similar experiences.
   c. at present, there is enormous uncertainty about the relationship between the activity in the brain and the ideas and thoughts available to introspection.
   d. participants' motivation might influence what they choose to disclose.

   Answer: c

10. Introspection, by definition, cannot be used to study:
    a. topics that are strongly colored by emotion.
    b. mental events that are unconscious.
    c. processes that involve conceptual knowledge.
    d. events that take a long time to unfold.

    Answer: b

11. Which of the following provides the most serious obstacle to the use of introspection as a source of scientific evidence?
    a. when facts are provided by introspection, we have no way to assess the facts themselves, independent of the reporter's particular perspective on the facts.
    b. introspection requires an alert, verbally expressive investigator; otherwise, the evidence provided by introspection will be of poor quality.
    c. introspection provides evidence about some mental events but cannot provide evidence about unconscious processes or ideas.
    d. the process of reporting on one's own mental events can take a lot of time, and can slow down the processes under investigation.

    Answer: a

12. Which of the following would a classical behaviorist be *least* likely to study?
    a. a participant's response to a particular situation
    b. a participant's beliefs
    c. changes in a participant's behavior that follow changes in the environment
    d. principles that apply equally to human behavior and to the behavior of other species.

    Answer: b

13. Historically, the movement known as behaviorism was encouraged by scholars' concerns regarding:
    a. psychotherapy.
    b. the discussion of the human mind as though it were some sort of computer.
    c. research based on introspection.
    d. a focus on brain mechanisms and a corresponding inattention to mental states.

    Answer: c

14. One important difference between classical behaviorism and cognitive psychology is that cognitive psychology:
    a. argues that unobservable mental states can be scientifically studied.
    b. rejects the use of human participants.
    c. insists on studying topics that can be directly and objectively observed.
    d. emphasizes the evolutionary roots of our behavior.

    Answer: a

15. Modern psychology turned away from behaviorism in its classic form because:
    a. our behavior is routinely determined by our understanding of stimuli.
    b. humans are more similar to computers than to other species studied in the laboratory.
    c. psychology rejected behaviorism's emphasis on an organism's subjective states.
    d. an organism's behavior can be changed by learning.

    Answer: a

16. The behaviorists argued that mentalistic processes or events could not be studied objectively; therefore, they chose instead to study organisms':
    a. expectations.
    b. desires and motivations.
    c. dreams.
    d. responses.

    Answer: d

17. If Sheila says, "Pass the salt, please," you are likely to pass her the salt. You'll probably respond in the same way if Sheila (a chemistry major) instead asks, "Could you please hand me the sodium chloride crystals?" This observation seems to indicate that our behavior:
    a. is primarily controlled by the physical characteristics of the stimuli we encounter.
    b. is shaped by the literal meanings of the stimuli we encounter.

c. is determined by simple associations among the stimuli we encounter.

d. is governed by what the stimuli we encounter mean to us.

Answer: d

18. Cognitive psychology often relies on the transcendental method, in which:
    a. mental events are explained by referring to events in the central nervous system.
    b. information from introspection transcends behavioral data.
    c. researchers seek to infer the properties of unseen events on the basis of the observable effects of those events.
    d. theories are tested via computer models.

Answer: c

19. The philosopher Immanuel Kant based many of his arguments on transcendental inferences. A commonplace example of such an inference is:
    a. a physicist inferring what the attributes of the electron must be based on visible effects caused by the electron.
    b. a computer scientist inferring what the attributes of a program must be based on her long-range goals for the program's functioning.
    c. a biologist inferring how an organism is likely to behave in the future based on assessment of past behaviors.
    d. a behaviorist inferring how a behavior was learned based on a deduction from well-established principles of learning.

Answer: a

20. Cognitive psychologists often discuss analogies between the mind's functioning and the functioning of a computer. These analogies:
    a. force researchers to phrase their theories in terms of the biology of the brain, analogous to the computer's hardware.
    b. force researchers to phrase their theories in terms of mental processes, analogous to the computer's software.
    c. force theories away from accounts that refer to beliefs, strategies, assumptions, and other mentalistic notions.
    d. permit explanations that refer to software or to hardware.

Answer: d

21. Consider the sentence "Sam, tired from hours of reading and working on his term paper, fell into bed at last." When you reach the sentence's thirteenth word ("fell"), you need to remember how the sentence began; otherwise, you won't know *who* fell into bed. The memory used for this task is called:
    a. episodic memory.
    b. working memory.

c. generic memory.

d. long-term memory.

Answer: b

22. In an experimental procedure, participants hear a sequence of letters, and then, a moment later, are required to repeat back the sequence. The longest sequence for which participants can easily do this is likely to contain _____ letters.

a. three

b. five

c. seven

d. twelve

Answer: c

23. A participant hears the sequence "F, D, P, U, G, Q, R" and then, a moment later, must repeat the sequence aloud. If errors occur in this procedure, they are likely:

a. to involve sound-alike confusions, e.g., repeating T instead of D.

b. to involve look-alike confusions, e.g., O instead of Q.

c. to involve confusions with "near neighbors" in the alphabet, e.g., repeating G instead of F.

d. to involve confusions in terms of strong associations, such as repeating I instead of Q because of the familiarity of "I.Q."

Answer: a

24. Theorists have proposed that working memory is best understood as a *system* involving multiple components. The activities of this system are controlled by a resource called:

a. the secretary.

b. the supervisor.

c. the central processor.

d. the central executive.

Answer: d

25. Within the working-memory system, mental "scratch pads" are available to allow storage of information soon to be needed but not currently in use. A crucial scratch pad is:

a. the output buffer.

b. the executive assistant.

c. the response planning system.

d. the articulatory rehearsal loop.

Answer: d

26. The technical term for "talking to yourself," when rehearsing verbal material is:
    a. vocal memory.
    b. schizophrenia.
    c. subvocalization.
    d. subconscious reading.

    Answer: c

27. In using the articulatory rehearsal loop, the central executive temporarily relies on storage:
    a. in a phonological buffer.
    b. in episodic memory.
    c. in a subvocal bank.
    d. in a visual form in visual memory.

    Answer: a

28. Participants in an experiment are shown a series of digits, and then asked to repeat them back a moment later. While being shown the sequence, the participants are required to say "tah, tah, tah" out loud, over and over. The evidence indicates that the recitation of "tah, tah, tah":
    a. will have no effect on participants' memory performance.
    b. will provide a rhythm that helps organize participants' rehearsal of the digits, thereby improving their memory performance.
    c. will block participants from using the inner voice to rehearse the digits, thereby interfering with the memory task.
    d. will force participants to rely on the central executive rather than on a less powerful lower level assistant, thereby improving memory performance.

    Answer: c

29. One group of participants is given a span test in which they are required to remember lists of one-syllable words (such as "top, cat, rock"). A second group is given a span test in which they must remember lists of two-syllable words ("topic, cattle, rocket"). Based on previous findings, we should predict:
    a. better performance for the first group because the one-syllable words can be more quickly pronounced and thus rehearsed more efficiently.
    b. equivalent performance for the two groups because memory depends primarily on the meaning of the words, not the particulars of the sound pattern.
    c. better performance for the second group because the two-syllable words provide a richer set of sound cues, promoting memory retrieval.
    d. better performance for the first group if testing follows immediately after the presentation of the words, and better performance for the second group if testing is delayed.

    Answer: a

30. Evidence from anarthric (speech-less) patients suggests that:
    a. muscles necessary for speech are also needed for subvocalization.
    b. subvocalization does not use words.
    c. muscles needed for speech are *not* needed for subvocalization.
    d. these patients are unable to subvocalize.

    Answer: c

31. Evidence from neuroimaging studies suggests that subvocalization is most closely related to:
    a. actually speaking out loud, because the same muscles are used.
    b. remembering a feeling.
    c. visual imagery.
    d. planning to speak, because some of the same brain regions are active as in normal speech planning.

    Answer: d

32. In a test of working memory capacity, participants are best able to remember:
    a. long words, because they contain more phonological information.
    b. short words, because they can be more efficiently rehearsed.
    c. abstract words, because they provide more opportunity for elaboration.
    d. rhyming words, because they are easily grouped together.

    Answer: b

CHAPTER 2 | The Neural Basis for Cognition

1. All of the following *may* be true of a person with Capgras Syndrome, *except*:
   a. she thinks that her mother has been replaced by a look-alike alien.
   b. she cannot recognize that her father looks like her father.
   c. she also has Alzheimer's Syndrome.
   d. she has no warm sense of familiarity when she sees a close friend.

   Answer: b

2. Some researchers explain Capgras Syndrome as:
   a. a simple failure of visual recognition.
   b. the result of a disconnection between a cognitive appraisal and a sense of familiarity.
   c. a subtype of schizophrenia.
   d. a failure of long-term memory, because patients cannot remember what their own close family members look like.

   Answer: b

3. Among its other functions, the amygdala seems to serve as:
   a. an important relay station between the eye and occipital cortex.
   b. a storage location for information received from the skin.
   c. an "emotional evaluator" or threat detector.
   d. an "index" for locating memories in the brain.

   Answer: c

4. A confabulation is:
   a. a type of lesion.
   b. a type of memory error.
   c. a perceptual problem caused by retinal damage.
   d. a neuroimaging technique.

   Answer: b

5. All of the following are true of confabulations, *except*:
   a. they are associated with right prefrontal cortex damage.
   b. they are generally sincere.
   c. they are in general wholly false.
   d. they are easy to identify because they lack the kind of detail found in other memories.

   Answer: d

6. The hindbrain is responsible for which of the following?
   a. rhythm of breathing, initiating sleep, posture
   b. complex thought, long-term memory
   c. planned motor activity
   d. perception and visual imagery

   Answer: a

7. The cortex makes up the surface of which brain structure?
   a. the hindbrain
   b. the midbrain
   c. the thalamus
   d. the forebrain

   Answer: d

8. The limbic system includes all of the following, *except*:
   a. the hippocampus.
   b. the amygdala.
   c. the cerebellum.
   d. the mammillary bodies.

   Answer: c

9. Commissures, including the corpus callosum, are:
   a. blood vessels that carry blood to all areas of the brain.
   b. brain areas associated with various types of sensory information.
   c. pockets of oxygen found throughout the brain.
   d. thick bundles of fibers that allow communication between the brain's hemispheres.

   Answer: d

10. Damage to the brain can be caused in many ways, but in general the damage is referred to as:
    a. a stroke.
    b. a lesion.
    c. a syndrome.
    d. an ablation.

    Answer: b

11. A number of techniques have been developed that allow us to examine the moment-by-moment activity levels of specifically defined brain areas. These techniques are called:
    a. EEG measurement.
    b. neuroimaging techniques.
    c. chronometric techniques.
    d. psychometric assessment.

    Answer: b

12. A CT or CAT (computerized axial tomography) scan:
    a. can only be performed on a cadaver.
    b. uses X rays to study the living brain's anatomy.
    c. is primarily useful for measuring blood flow in the brain.
    d. can detect the activity taking place in different brain areas in real time.

    Answer: b

13. PET (positron emission tomography) scans show:
    a. minute details of brain anatomy.
    b. what a participant is thinking at the moment the test is taken.
    c. brain areas that are currently consuming a particularly high level of glucose.
    d. whether a participant is learning something new or remembering prior learning.

    Answer: c

14. An MRI (magnetic resonance imaging) or fMRI (functional magnetic-resonance imaging):
    a. is less useful than other types of neuroimaging for the study of the functioning of the brain.
    b. creates a three-dimensional representation of the brain's tissue.
    c. is useful only for studying features on the outer surface of the brain.
    d. makes self-report data unnecessary.

    Answer: b

15. If a researcher applies mild electrical current to a specific area of an animal's right hemisphere primary motor projection area, which of the following is likely to happen?
    a. a specific movement of a body part on the right side of the animal.
    b. a specific movement of a body part on the left side of the animal.
    c. a chaotic movement of the entire animal.
    d. no movement at all.

    Answer: b

16. The auditory cortex follows the principle of contralateral control. Thus,
    a. the right temporal lobe receives most of its input from the left ear.
    b. the right temporal lobe receives most of its input from the right ear.
    c. the right temporal lobe receives equal input from both ears.
    d. the information received by the right temporal lobe depends on whether the listener favors their right or left ear.

    Answer: a

17. The primary motor projection area is located:
    a. in the cerebellum.
    b. in the occipital cortex.
    c. toward the rear of the frontal lobe.
    d. in the midbrain.

    Answer: c

18. Motor and sensory cortices combined make up what portion of the brain?
    a. less than 10 percent.
    b. roughly 25 percent.
    c. just over 50 percent.
    d. nearly 85 percent.

    Answer: b

19. A patient with visual agnosia will probably show an inability to:
    a. remember a list of words heard one hour before.
    b. detect brief flashes of light.
    c. recall the color of familiar objects (e.g., that stop signs are red).
    d. identify common objects in plain view.

    Answer: d

20. Injury to the brain, such as a stroke, can impair people's ability to recognize patterns. This inability is known as:
    a. agnosia.
    b. aphasia.
    c. functional blindness.
    d. a hemispheric lesion.

    Answer: a

21. Toby and Tim both have lesions in their left frontal lobes. Toby has trouble producing speech; Tim has difficulties comprehending speech. Both Toby and Tim are likely to receive a diagnosis of:
    a. neglect syndrome.
    b. apraxia.
    c. agnosia.
    d. aphasia.

    Answer: d

22. Damage to the prefrontal area leads to:
    a. neglect syndrome.
    b. a variety of problems, including problems planning and implementing strategies.
    c. exclusively difficulties with memory.
    d. primarily language problems.

    Answer: b

23. Rods and cones are different in all of the following respects, *except*:
    a. rods are sensitive to lower levels of light.
    b. only cones are able to discriminate color (hue).
    c. there are three types of rods (for three different wavelengths of light) and only one type of cone.
    d. cones have greater acuity.

    Answer: c

24. The fovea is all of the following, *except*:
    a. a cluster of cones in the center of the retina.
    b. the so-called blind-spot.
    c. the region of the retina with the greatest acuity.
    d. the area of the retina on which we place a target image in order to see the target clearly.

    Answer: b

25. The lateral geniculate nucleus (LGN) is:
    a. a way station between the eye and the occipital cortex, located in the thalamus.
    b. an important area in the amygdala, associated with long-term memory.
    c. the section of the optic nerve closest to the eye.
    d. the location in the temporal cortex where auditory information is stored.

    Answer: a

26. Cells A and B are receiving the same high levels of stimulation, but Cell A is showing a lower level of activity than Cell B. A likely explanation for this fact is:
    a. Cell A is defective.
    b. Cell A is receiving input from the edge of a surface, while Cell B is receiving input from a portion of the surface away from the edge.
    c. Cell A is being laterally inhibited by other nearby cells.
    d. Cell A has a higher resting level than Cell B.

    Answer: c

27. Cells detecting the boundary of a surface are subject to less lateral inhibition than cells detecting the center of the same surface. This leads to an effect called:
    a. lateral enhancement.
    b. edge enhancement.
    c. the boundary rule.
    d. the all-or-none law.

    Answer: b

28. A neuron is:
    a. a group of cells specialized for a particular type of information storage.
    b. one of the fibers connecting the eye to the visual cortex.
    c. an individual cell within the nervous system
    d. a region within the brain dedicated to a single function.

    Answer: c

29. A researcher wishes to determine exactly when a particular neuron is firing. A technique well suited to this purpose is:
    a. neuropsychological testing.
    b. lesion studies.
    c. stereotaxis.
    d. single-cell recording.

    Answer: d

30. Once a cell fires, the part of a neuron that transmits information to another location is:
    a. the dendrite.
    b. the cell body.
    c. the axon.
    d. the nucleus.

    Answer: c

31. A synapse is:
    a. a message sent from one neuron to another.
    b. part of a neuron's cell body.
    c. made up of the end of one neuron's axon, another neuron's receiving membrane, and the gap between these.
    d. the name of the electrical signal that occurs when a cell reaches its threshold.

    Answer: c

32. A neuron's initial, internal response to an incoming signal can vary in size. The ultimate, external response of the cell, however, does not vary in size.

If the signal is sent, it is always of the same magnitude. This effect is called:
a. the whole-firing potential.
b. the all-or-none law.
c. the uniform response law.
d. the threshold potential.

Answer: b

33. A researcher wishes to define the receptive field for a particular neuron in the visual cortex. To do this, the researcher will need to specify:
a. the portion of the neuron that receives input from neighboring neurons.
b. an area within the visual field, with the cell firing if the appropriate target appears within the area.
c. where the neuron is located within the visual cortex.
d. the brain area from which the neuron is receiving its input.

Answer: b

34. A researcher has identified the receptive field for a neuron and has determined that the receptive field has a center-surround organization. If the researcher were to shine light into the entire receptive field, including both the center and the surrounding area, we would expect:
a. the neuron to continue firing at its resting rate.
b. the neuron to increase its firing rate.
c. the neuron to decrease its firing rate.
d. the neuron to cease firing.

Answer: a

35. The specialization evident in visual processing shows that:
a. the visual system relies on parallel processing.
b. all of the various aspects of visual processing occur within the occipital cortex.
c. the visual system relies exclusively on serial processing.
d. all visual processing occurs in the right hemisphere.

Answer: a

36. Visual agnosia is associated with damage to which of the following:
a. Area V1
b. the "where" system, which carries information from the occipital cortex to the parietal cortex
c. the "what" system, which carries information from the occipital cortex to the temporal cortex
d. Area MT

Answer: c

37. Patients who have suffered damage to the occipital-parietal pathway (the "where" system) will have difficulties with which of the following tasks?
    a. visually identifying a toothbrush on the counter in front of them
    b. describing the function of the toothbrush without touching it
    c. reaching in the correct direction to retrieve the toothbrush
    d. knowing how to use the toothbrush once they have retrieved it

    Answer: c

38. Human brains have a distinct division-of-labor strategy. Each task is achieved as a result of multiple brain areas working together. But the work of the various parts of the brain must be compiled into a finished whole. The issue of how this reassembly works is referred to as:
    a. the binding problem.
    b. the Humpty Dumpty dilemma.
    c. the reassembly law.
    d. the ultimate puzzle.

    Answer: a

CHAPTER 3 | Recognizing Objects in the World

1. Which of the following is not an example of pattern recognition?
   a. "I smell smoke; is something burning?"
   b. "Oh, look! There's a blue heron!"
   c. "The moment I heard the performance, I knew it was a piece by Bach."
   d. "I remember that a sextant is a type of navigational instrument."

   Answer: d

2. In order to summarize the Gestalt psychologists' movement in a few words, one might say:
   a. "If you can't see it happen, it isn't worth studying."
   b. "The perceptual whole is different than the sum of its parts."
   c. "All that is important happens in the subconscious."
   d. "What you see is what you get."

   Answer: b

3. The importance of vision for humans is reflected in:
   a. the close proximity of the eyes to the visual cortex.
   b. the inability of brain damage to disrupt the visual system.
   c. the lack of a "blind spot" in humans.
   d. the relative size of the visual cortex.

   Answer: d

4. Recognizing a visual pattern often depends on how you *parse* the stimulus input. "Parsing" refers to:
   a. which side of the form you perceive as its *top*.
   b. the viewing distance you take in perceiving the form.
   c. the process by which you dissect the form into its appropriate pieces.
   d. the name you associate with the particular pattern.

   Answer: c

5. One might propose that pattern recognition begins with the identification of simple elements; these are then added together, like tiles within a mosaic, to allow recognition of the large-scale pattern. Of the following, which is *most problematic* for this proposal?
   a. The elements identified within a pattern can be changed dramatically by a change in context.
   b. Patterns can be identified even if viewed from a novel distance.
   c. Many variations on a single pattern can be recognized, despite differences from one variation to the next.
   d. Patterns can be identified even if viewed from a novel orientation.

   Answer: a

6. Which of the following is *not* true for feature-based models of pattern recognition?
   a. Features, as general-purpose building blocks, can help explain how humans recognize variations on a form (e.g., a cat in different positions, or a letter in different type fonts).
   b. The visual system identifies small pieces of a pattern first and then combines them to form more complex wholes.
   c. Search tasks are generally easier if a single feature distinguishes the target from other items in the field.
   d. While functional and computational models have made clear the advantages of a feature-based system, we have not yet located the mechanisms in the brain that might support such a system.

   Answer: d

7. In a visual search task, participants are most likely to search quickly for a target if:
   a. the target is defined by a combination of features rather than by a single feature.
   b. the target can be distinguished from the background items on the basis of a single feature.
   c. the target and the background items have many features in common.
   d. all the items in view are arranged in an orderly pattern.

   Answer: b

8. Which of the following is an example of a "search asymmetry"?
   a. It is easier to locate an asymmetrical target (such as J or K) than it is to locate a symmetrical target (such as M or O).
   b. It is easier to locate a target if one searches through the field in a left-to-right direction than it is if one searches in the opposite direction.
   c. It is easier to locate a vertical line among a field of tilted lines than it is to locate a single tilted line among a field of vertical lines.

d. It is difficult to find a single symmetrical target among a field of asymmetrical items.

Answer: c

9. Search asymmetries can be interpreted as evidence for which of the following claims?
   a. An occurrence of an element (such as a gap) can constitute a feature for the visual system, even though the absence of that element (no gap) does not constitute a feature.
   b. The perceptual system pays special attention to symmetrical targets, indicating that symmetry is one of the features of great importance in pattern recognition.
   c. In general, if a feature can be recognized swiftly by the visual system, so can the mirror image of that feature.
   d. Virtually any visual configuration can be used as a feature, provided that the configuration is not too complex.

Answer: a

10. A tachistoscope is a device used to:
    a. measure the rate at which a neuron is firing.
    b. provide precise measurements of reaction times.
    c. display stimuli briefly.
    d. record the moment-by-moment activities of the brain.

Answer: c

11. If a task is too easy, *all* participants will do well in the task, and therefore the task cannot be used to determine which participants do the task easily, and which do it with difficulty. In this case:
    a. the task is not valid because the performance measures are likely to be unreliable.
    b. the task is degraded because performance is at baseline levels.
    c. the task is not valid because performance will show a threshold pattern.
    d. the task provides an insensitive measure because performance is too close to the ceiling.

Answer: d

12. In tachistoscopic studies, a poststimulus mask is usually employed to:
    a. disrupt sensory memory.
    b. prevent verbalization.
    c. help the participants maintain proper eye position.
    d. discourage guessing about the stimulus.

Answer: a

13. In a tachistoscopic procedure, a word is likely to be more difficult to recognize if:
    a. it is a word the participant has encountered recently.
    b. it is a word used frequently in the language.
    c. the word has an unusual spelling pattern.
    d. the word is semantically related to a recently presented word.

    Answer: c

14. Participants' recognition thresholds are:
    a. lower for frequently seen words.
    b. higher for recently seen words.
    c. not affected by priming.
    d. lower for highly unusual words.

    Answer: a

15. Participants are shown a visual stimulus for just 30 msec and are then asked, "Was there an E or a K in the stimulus?" We would expect the best performance if the stimulus was:
    a. BARK
    b. K
    c. BWQK
    d. GALK

    Answer: a

16. A participant reads a list of words, and the word "elephant" appears several times in that list. Later, the participant tachistoscopically views another list of words. When the word "elephant" appears in the second list, the participant's response rate is faster than for other words not found on the previous list. This effect is called:
    a. the word-superiority effect.
    b. the redundancy claim.
    c. working memory availability.
    d. repetition priming.

    Answer: d

17. The "word-superiority effect" refers to the fact that:
    a. short (three- or four-letter) words are easier to recognize than longer words.
    b. it is easier to recognize a letter within the context of a word than it is to recognize a letter presented by itself.
    c. it is easier to recognize a word presented in a phrase than it is to recognize a word presented by itself.
    d. words that are frequently used are more readily identified under tachistoscopic conditions.

    Answer: b

18. The "word-superiority effect" refers to the fact that:
    a. words are easier to perceive than intact phrases even if the phrases are highly familiar.
    b. a letter is more easily recognized if presented within a word than it is if presented in isolation.
    c. recognition of a letter is not facilitated if the letter appears in a nonword string even if the string follows the rules of English spelling.
    d. words are more easily recognized in isolation than within a sentence.

    Answer: b

19. In a tachistoscopic procedure, participants are shown the sequence "NACL." Evidence indicates that:
    a. the distinctive letter pattern in the sequence will help participants recognize the sequence.
    b. the familiarity of the sequence (the chemical formula for table salt) will help participants recognize the sequence.
    c. participants are likely to misperceive the sequence, reading it as if it were a common letter pattern such as "NAIL."
    d. participants will be unable to organize the letters, and therefore they will only perceive some of the sequence's features, not the large-scale units.

    Answer: c

20. In tachistoscopic recognition, participants often make "over-regularization" errors. These are errors in which:
    a. participants perceive a word as pertaining to their personal experiences even when the word is relatively neutral.
    b. participants perceive a word as being related to the previous word when in fact it is not.
    c. participants are shown a frequently used word but perceive it as an infrequently used word.
    d. participants are shown a pattern such as "MJLK" but perceive it as "MILK."

    Answer: d

21. A feature net is:
    a. a network of detectors organized in layers, with one of the lower levels of detectors specialized for detecting features.
    b. a collective of features used to describe an object's form.
    c. a net-like structure of brain cells designed to detect features.
    d. a conceptualization of how features are visually related to one another.

    Answer: a

22. Compared to detectors that *haven't* fired recently, a detector that *has* fired recently is likely:
    a. to be at a higher position within the network of detectors.
    b. to have a higher response threshold.
    c. to have a higher activation level.
    d. to require more priming in order to fire.

    Answer: c

23. A bigram detector fires in response to the:
    a. appropriate object weight.
    b. appropriately shaped curve.
    c. appropriately positioned corner.
    d. appropriate letter pair.

    Answer: d

24. A response threshold is:
    a. the exposure duration for which a word must be displayed tachistoscopically for a particular participant to perceive it.
    b. the number of correct responses required in order for a participant to be above floor on a particular task.
    c. the amount of certainty or conviction a participant expresses when selecting a particular response.
    d. the activation level at which a response occurs.

    Answer: d

25. English-like nonwords (e.g., "HICE") are easier to *perceive* than strings of letters not resembling English (e.g., "RSFK") because:
    a. they are encountered more often.
    b. bigram-detectors for more common letter combinations fire more readily.
    c. they are more distinctive.
    d. word-detectors will respond to near-words as well as true words.

    Answer: b

26. On one trial of an experiment, a participant is shown the sequence "GWXT." On a different trial, the participant is shown the sequence "PAFE." Based on prior research, we should expect that:
    a. "PAFE" will be easier to perceive than "GWXT" because detectors for "PA" and "FE" are likely to be well primed.
    b. the letter sequences will be equally difficult to perceive because neither is a word.
    c. participants will perceive more of the letters in "GWXT" because they are likely to confuse "PAFE" with "PACE" or "SAFE."

d. the letter sequences will be equally difficult to perceive because both contain regular bigram patterns.

Answer: a

27. Participants in a tachistoscopic procedure are shown the sequence "CQRN." Participants misperceive this string as "CORN." In a feature-net account, which of the following is probably *not* contributing to this effect?
   a. O is a more frequent letter in English than is Q. Therefore, the O detector is better primed.
   b. "CO" is a more frequent letter pair in English than is "CQ." Therefore, the "CO" detector is better primed.
   c. A well-primed bigram detector will fire even if the letter detectors feeding into that bigram detector are firing weakly.
   d. Feature nets are generally unable to identify nonwords.

Answer: d

28. In a feature-net model, knowledge of spelling patterns:
   a. can influence the perception of whole words but not the perception of single letters or bigrams.
   b. is distributed across the model, and therefore the knowledge is only detectable in the overall functioning of the network.
   c. is locally represented, allowing the network to draw inferences about partially viewed stimuli.
   d. is overshadowed by the parallel processing employed by the net.

Answer: b

29. The chapter describes in detail *one way* a feature net can be designed, but other designs may turn out to be preferable. For example, more recent hypotheses, including McClelland and Rumelhart's model, make use of all of the following *except*:
   a. inhibitory connections among the detectors.
   b. the elimination of feature detectors, relying instead on geon detectors.
   c. connections allowing detectors at one level in the network to influence detectors at lower levels.
   d. connections allowing detectors at one level in the network to influence other detectors at the same level.

Answer: b

30. Biederman's Recognition by Components (RBC) model:
   a. does not rely on a hierarchy of detectors.
   b. makes use of geon detectors, which in turn trigger detectors for geon assemblies.
   c. asserts that priming takes place primarily at levels higher than the level of geon detectors.

    d. can recognize three-dimensional objects provided they are seen from the appropriate viewing angle.

Answer: b

31. We can often recognize an object even if some of the object's parts are hidden from view. Evidence indicates that this "recognition from partial viewing" will be easiest if:
    a. we can see enough of the object to identify some of its geons.
    b. we can see at least 20 percent of the object's features.
    c. the object's features are unfamiliar to us so that there is no risk of false alarms.
    d. the object does not have too many geons.

Answer: a

32. When we proofread a paper, we sometimes perceive letters that are not there, thereby failing to detect spelling errors on the page. A similar phenomenon, perceiving aspects of the stimulus that are not actually present, has been documented in hearing. This phenomenon is called:
    a. the biased-perceiver effect.
    b. the word-frequency effect.
    c. the verbal-transformation effect.
    d. the restoration effect.

Answer: d

33. Speed-reading:
    a. involves collecting more information from a page of text than one does in normal reading.
    b. uses more stable, continuous eye movements to allow the eye to move across each line of text more smoothly.
    c. employs the same mechanisms as normal reading, only with *less* actual perception and *more* inference.
    d. is more useful than slower reading for picking up details in the text, because a speed-reader has less time to get bored.

Answer: c

34. Studies of hearing indicate that:
    a. our auditory perception is generally more accurate than our visual perception.
    b. auditory perception is influenced by large-scale configurations, in contrast to the feature base evident in visual perception.
    c. our knowledge of common sound patterns can influence what we perceive.
    d. our auditory perception does not depend on feature detection.

Answer: c

35. The form of brain damage identified as prosopagnosia is primarily characterized by:
    a. an inability to recognize faces.
    b. an inability to comprehend written text.
    c. an inability to identify inverted stimuli even though perception of upright stimuli seems normal.
    d. an inability to identify familiar voices.

    Answer: a

36. The recognition of faces:
    a. seems to rely on the detection of features and geons, indicating that the recognition by components model can be applied to face recognition.
    b. resembles other forms of recognition in that our ability to recognize faces is relatively unimpaired by changes in viewing angle or orientation.
    c. differs from other forms of recognition in that face recognition appears not to be influenced by expectation or knowledge effects.
    d. is influenced by configurational factors, suggesting that a model based on feature detection will provide a poor explanation of face recognition.

    Answer: d

37. "Bottom-up" (or "data-driven") mechanisms refer to:
    a. the scientific process in which all claims must be rooted in well-established biological evidence.
    b. mechanisms for which activity is primarily triggered and shaped by the incoming stimulus information.
    c. mechanisms for which activity is influenced by thoughts provided by the individual.
    d. the process by which researchers seek to develop new theories by paying close attention to the available data.

    Answer: b

38. It is easier to read the sequence "The boy ran" than it is to read the sequence "Ran boy the." This observation indicates that:
    a. word recognition depends on the same mechanisms as letter recognition.
    b. word recognition, like letter recognition, is facilitated by a well-formed context.
    c. word recognition can not be accomplished by "top-down" (or concept-driven) mechanisms alone.
    d. the visual system needs to have word-pair detectors, analogous to bigram detectors, with detectors for frequent word pairs being particularly well primed.

    Answer: b

CHAPTER 4 | Paying Attention

1. The task of shadowing involves:
   a. repeating, word for word, the contents of a (usually tape-recorded) message.
   b. drawing the mirror image of a simple drawing.
   c. copying the movements of a target individual.
   d. repeating back, from memory, a message heard some minutes earlier.

   Answer: a

2. Tasks involving dichotic listening are tasks in which:
   a. two different visual stimuli are presented.
   b. two different auditory messages are presented, one to each ear.
   c. participants must identify subthreshold sounds.
   d. participants must dichotomize sounds into distinct categories.

   Answer: b

3. A participant has just participated in an experiment involving dichotic listening. Of the following, the participant is *least likely* to remember:
   a. whether the unattended channel was spoken by a male or a female.
   b. whether the unattended channel contained nonspeech noises or speech.
   c. the semantic content of the attended channel.
   d. the meaning of the words presented on the unattended channel.

   Answer: d

4. In dichotic listening tasks, participants are able to:
   a. tell if the unattended channel contained a coherent message or just random words.
   b. identify physical attributes of the message on the unattended channel.
   c. concentrate effectively on the attended channel, so they end up detecting nothing on the unattended channel.

    d. maintain their focus on the attended channel only with considerable difficulty and frequent slips.

Answer: b

5. A participant is asked to shadow a message presented to the left ear while simultaneously ignoring a message presented to the right ear. During the experiment, which of the following is the participant *least likely* to detect?
    a. The right ear's message is initially presented in a high-pitched voice but is then spoken by a low-pitched voice.
    b. The participant's name is mentioned three times at various points within the right ear's message.
    c. Initially, the right ear's message contains a male voice reading a coherent passage, but this is then replaced by the same voice reading a sequence of random words.
    d. The right ear's message is identical to the left ear's message but lags behind the attended message by a few seconds.

Answer: c

6. In dichotic listening experiments, some aspects of the unattended message seem to leak through and are heard despite the participant's intention to ignore the message. Which of the following is *un*likely to leak through in this fashion?
    a. material that is easily distinguishable from the attended message in its semantic content
    b. mention of the participant's own name
    c. mention of a topic of personal importance to the participant
    d. material that is identical to what was heard a second or two earlier on the attended channel

Answer: a

7. Participants are shown a series of letters and are asked to name aloud the letters printed in red. On trial 18, the participants are shown a red R superimposed on a green G. On trial 19, the letter printed in red is a G. Evidence indicates that we should expect:
    a. a faster response to the G because this letter was just seen on the previous trial.
    b. a slowed response to the G because this letter was just ignored on the previous trial.
    c. no effect from G's presence in trial 18 because the G was not attended on that previous trial.
    d. a faster response to the G if participants happened to have noticed it on the previous trial, but otherwise no effect.

Answer: b

8. Participants are instructed to fixate on a point on a computer screen and report on a "+" that appears off to one side. After several trials, the fixation point is replaced by a new shape, but the participants do not notice this change. This is a study of:
   a. inattention blindness.
   b. neglect syndrome.
   c. attentional apathy.
   d. shadowing.

   Answer: a

9. If one interprets dichotic-listening results in terms of "limited processing resources," which of the following claims fits *least well* with the data?
   a. The detection of a message's semantic content relies on well-practiced activities, and therefore the detection places a minimal demand on our processing resources.
   b. Participants generally fail to perceive the unattended message simply because they have not devoted enough resources to the processing of this message.
   c. Participants occasionally perceive elements of the unattended message, and they tend to be elements that can be detected with minimal resources.
   d. Participants do not have the option of perceiving both the attended and unattended message, since this would require more resources than are available.

   Answer: a

10. To explain dichotic listening data in terms of "limited mental resources," we would need to argue that:
    a. participants do not have adequate resources available for processing the meaning of the attended channel.
    b. no resources are required for the comprehension of a single message, but the comprehension of two messages creates a large demand for resources.
    c. the physical attributes of the unattended channel can be identified via processes that require few resources.
    d. comprehension of the attended channel requires 100 percent of the participants' available resources.

    Answer: c

11. Performance in a shadowing task is improved if:
    a. the stimulus message is spoken by a voice similar to the participant's own voice.
    b. the distractor message is presented through a loudspeaker close in space to the source of the attended message.

c. the stimulus message is exciting.

d. the stimulus message is predictable.

Answer: d

12. In which of the following situations would we expect the fastest response time?

a. The stimulus being presented to the participant is identical in form to the stimulus used as the warning signal.

b. The stimulus being presented to the participant is markedly different from the stimulus used as the warning signal.

c. The stimulus being presented to the participant is the stimulus the participant was expecting.

d. The stimulus being presented to the participant is identical in form to the warning signal but is different from the stimulus the participant was expecting.

Answer: c

13. The different forms of priming can be distinguished in several ways. For example, the effects of _____ can be observed almost immediately after the relevant cue is provided; in contrast, the effects of _____ require a half-second or so to appear after the relevant cue.

a. concept-driven priming; data-driven priming

b. data-driven priming; concept-driven priming

c. expectation-based priming; repetition priming

d. semantic priming; repetition priming

Answer: b

14. Priming based on specific expectations about the identity of the upcoming stimulus produces:

a. no benefit for processing if the expectations are correct but slows processing if the expectations are incorrect.

b. a benefit for processing if the expectations are correct but slows processing if the expectations are incorrect.

c. a benefit for processing if the expectations are correct but has no effect on processing if the expectations are incorrect.

d. the same benefit as stimulus-based repetition priming.

Answer: b

15. Chronometric analysis exploits the fact that:

a. thinking is poorer "out loud."

b. women are faster than men on some memory tasks.

c. age influences memory capacity.

d. mental tasks take time.

Answer: d

16. In each trial of an experiment, participants see a warning signal and then, a half-second later, see a pair of letters. The participants press one button if the letters are the same (e.g., "W W") and a different button if the letters are different (e.g., "P X"). On 80 percent of the trials, the warning signal is identical to the letters that will be shown on that trial. Listed below are the warning signals and the test stimuli presented on trial number 97 of the procedure:

> Group 1   warning signal = "L" test pair = "L L"
> Group 2   warning signal = "U" test pair = "L L"
> Group 3   warning signal = "+" test pair = "L L"

In this setup we should expect:
   a. fastest responses from Group 3 and slowest responses from Group 2.
   b. fastest responses from Group 1 and slowest responses from Group 3.
   c. fastest responses from Group 1 and slowest responses from Group 2.
   d. fastest responses from Group 1 and no difference between Groups 2 and 3.

Answer: c

17. Some researchers have compared visual attention to a search-light beam sweeping across the visual field. Which of the following claims about this "beam" is *not* correct?
   a. It is possible to split the beam of visual attention, so that two nonadjacent positions are both within the beam.
   b. It is possible to redirect visual attention without changing the position of one's eyes.
   c. The beam of visual attention can be adjusted by the participant, so that the beam is sometimes wide, and sometimes narrow.
   d. Stimuli inside the beam of visual attention are processed more efficiently.

Answer: a

18. All of the following are true of the anterior attention system (AAS), *except*:
   a. it is exclusively responsible for the "search-light beam" quality of attention.
   b. it is the attention "traffic director," coordinating activities and inputs.
   c. it is tied to brain areas associated with working memory.
   d. it is tied to brain areas associated with initiation of action.

Answer: a

19. The available data indicate that:
   a. the brain mechanisms controlling attention are difficult to distinguish from the brain mechanisms directly involved in perception.
   b. multiple brain mechanisms are responsible for the control of attention.

c. a single mechanism governs the ability to disengage attention from its current focus and also the ability to lock in to a new attention focus.

d. the mechanisms controlling attention differ from one individual to the next.

Answer: b

20. A patient has suffered brain damage and, as a result, now seems to ignore all information on the left side of her world. If shown words, she only reads the right half of the word; if asked to copy a picture, she only copies the right half. This patient seems to be suffering from:
a. a hemispherectomy.
b. right hemiblindness.
c. the unilateral neglect syndrome.
d. parietal syndrome.

Answer: c

21. All of the following are true of patients with unilateral neglect syndrome, *except*:
a. in general, they seem to ignore half of the world.
b. when their attention is directed toward a particular object, it generally stays with that object.
c. if an object previously attended to is moved into the ignored half of the world, patients will start to ignore the object.
d. in bad cases, patients are unaware of the problem and thus make no attempt to compensate for it.

Answer: c

22. If a participant is asked to perform two activities at the same time, performance will be improved if:
a. the two activities are highly dissimilar, drawing on different task-specific resources.
b. the two activities are highly similar, drawing on the same task-specific resources.
c. both activities require large amounts of task-general resources.
d. neither activity involves verbal processing.

Answer: a

23. Participants are asked to listen to a tape-recorded message and to shadow the message as they hear it. Which of the following tasks will be easiest to combine with this shadowing task?
a. viewing a series of printed words, followed by a test measuring memory for the words
b. hearing a simultaneous tape-recorded message, followed by a test measuring memory for the gist of the second message

    c. hearing a simultaneous tape-recorded list of words, followed by a test measuring memory for the word list

    d. viewing a series of pictures, followed by a test measuring memory for the pictures

Answer: d

24. The existence of task-general resources is indicated by the fact that:
    a. similar tasks will interfere with each other more than dissimilar tasks.
    b. if a task has been heavily practiced, it is less likely to cause interference with other tasks.
    c. some brain lesions disrupt all tasks requiring attention.
    d. interference between two tasks can sometimes be observed even if the two tasks have no elements in common.

Answer: d

25. It has been hypothesized that some mental resources are unitary and therefore are not divisible. If two tasks both require one of these unitary resources, divided attention between these two tasks:
    a. will not be possible.
    b. will only be possible by means of time-sharing of the resource.
    c. will only be possible if the two tasks make different uses of the resource.
    d. will only be possible if the two tasks make matched demands of the resource.

Answer: b

26. The term "time-sharing" refers to:
    a. a phenomenon in which a single resource is used simultaneously by two different tasks.
    b. a strategy in which working memory is used to hold materials from two different sources.
    c. a process in which one rapidly switches attention from one task to another.
    d. a skill in performing two tasks at the same time.

Answer: c

27. The additional time required to make response B, if stimulus B is presented while the participant is still "working on" the response to stimulus A, is called:
    a. a psychological refractory period.
    b. a second-response delay.
    c. a serial processing error.
    d. an error in divided attention.

Answer: a

28. In an experimental procedure, participants are shown either an A or a B on a computer screen and then, a moment later, are shown a number. Participants must immediately respond to indicate which letter they've just seen and which number was presented. In this situation, we should expect that:
   a. if the number appears soon after the letter, participants' response to the number will be much slower than the participants' response to the letter.
   b. participants' response to the number will be faster than their response to the letter, thanks to response priming.
   c. participants' response to the letter will be faster than their response to the number, thanks to negative priming.
   d. if the number appears soon after the letter, participants will be able to rely on parallel processing and will respond equally quickly to both.

Answer: a

29. It has been claimed that many mental tasks rely on a unitary, general-purpose, nondivisible response selector. With this claim in mind, consider the following situation: Participants are shown a stimulus and then, a moment later, are shown a second stimulus. The participants' task is to respond to *both* stimuli, indicating the identity of each. We would expect that:
   a. the response to the second stimulus will be faster than the response to the first stimulus because the first response will "warm up" the selector.
   b. the presence of the second stimulus will slow down responding to the first stimulus.
   c. the response to the second stimulus may be slowed, since the response cannot be initiated until the selector is done with the first stimulus.
   d. the perception of the second stimulus may be slowed, since the perceptual activity must wait until the selector is done with the first stimulus.

Answer: c

30. Participants are asked to search for a particular target amidst a set of stimuli. On some trials two stimuli are presented, and participants must determine if one of them is the target. On other trials, *eight* stimuli are presented, and participants again must search for the target within the set. If participants are able to use a *parallel search* in this task, we would predict that:
   a. response times will be approximately four times slower in the trials with eight stimuli as compared with the trials with two stimuli.
   b. response times will be slower when searching through eight stimuli, but the information provided does not allow a prediction of how much slower they will be.
   c. response times will be faster when searching through the eight stimuli than when searching through the two stimuli.
   d. response times will be the same for searching through two stimuli and for searching through eight.

Answer: d

31. Participants are given practice in a search task with *varied mapping* between stimuli and responses. Under these circumstances, we would expect that after practice:
    a. participants' response times will not depend on the number of stimuli shown in each trial.
    b. participants will have great difficulty if the categorization of targets and distractors is now reversed.
    c. searching for the target will become automatic.
    d. participants must still use a serial search to locate the target on each trial.

    Answer: d

32. On trial 18 of a task, participants must search for the target F. An F is presented, and so the participants respond "yes." On trial 19 of the same procedure, participants must search for the target D. An F is presented, and so the participants respond "no." This task clearly involves:
    a. varied mapping.
    b. consistent mapping.
    c. Stroop interference.
    d. crosstalk.

    Answer: a

33. An experienced driver can drive while holding a relatively complex conversation. This combination of activities is difficult, however, for a novice driver. One way to explain this contrast relies on the assertion that:
    a. the two activities are very different, so the task combination creates no problems with channel segregation.
    b. practice of a task leads to a decline in the resource demands for the task.
    c. the two activities are very different, so they rely on different sets of task-specific resources.
    d. practice of the tasks diminishes the need for task-specific resources.

    Answer: b

34. A participant is shown a series of stimuli and is asked to name the color of the ink in which the stimuli are printed. The eighth stimulus happens to be printed in green ink. We should expect a relatively slow response if the stimulus happens to be:
    a. a series of green X's.
    b. the word "RED" printed in green.
    c. the participant's name printed in green.
    d. the word "GREEN" printed in green.

    Answer: b

35. Stroop interference indicates that:
    a. word reading is automatized.
    b. the identification of a stimulus requires few resources.

   c. practice with a variable-mapping task leads to automaticity.

   d. automatic activities cannot produce interference with other, simultaneous activities.

Answer: a

36. Automatic activities seem not to be reflexes in any literal sense, and this has led researchers to speak of automaticity as being "contingent." Which of the following observations illustrates this sort of contingency?
   a. Some activities, by virtue of their complexity, cannot be automatized.
   b. Automaticity does not depend on practice; instead, with the appropriate instruction, participants can behave in an automatized fashion in their first performance of a task.
   c. An action, once started, might proceed automatically, but the launching of the action is under the participant's control.
   d. An action will become automatized only if the action has been practiced in the appropriate fashion.

Answer: c

37. It appears that participants can learn to read a story while copying down different material being dictated to them. Nevertheless:
   a. this is possible only if both of the tasks have a consistent mapping from inputs to responses.
   b. participants will fail to grasp the meaning of the material they are reading.
   c. only exceptional participants are able to acquire this skill.
   d. participants need to practice doing the two tasks together, as opposed to practicing each of the tasks on its own.

Answer: d

38. "Crosstalk" between two tasks is defined as:
   a. leakage of information about one of the tasks into the processing of the other task.
   b. integration of the information received from more than one source.
   c. assimilation of information received in one context into a new context.
   d. focus on the contrasts between two tasks.

Answer: a

39. Performance in divided-attention tasks is limited by several different factors. Which of the following is not one of those limits?
   a. the participant's ability to segregate the two channels
   b. the demands of the combined tasks for task-general resources
   c. the participant's ability to promote crosstalk
   d. the demands of the combined tasks for task-specific resources

Answer: c

CHAPTER 5 | The Acquisition of Memories

1. The operations through which we gain new knowledge, retain that knowledge, and later use that knowledge are often divided into three categories. Which of the following is *not* one of those categories?
   a. retrieval
   b. acquisition
   c. deliberation
   d. storage

   Answer: c

2. Which of the following is *not* an attribute of working memory (sometimes called short-term memory)?
   a. unlimited storage capacity
   b. drawn on by a wide range of tasks
   c. easily accessible
   d. contents closely associated with the current focus of attention

   Answer: a

3. One difference between *working memory* and *long-term memory* is that:
   a. the contents of working memory tend to be in the form of visual images, whereas the contents of long-term memory are often verbal and symbolic.
   b. damage to the brain can disrupt working memory, but long-term memory seems not to be similarly vulnerable.
   c. the contents of working memory last only a half-second or so, whereas the contents of long-term memory are much more durable.
   d. the contents of working memory depend on the content of one's current thinking; the contents of long-term memory do not.

   Answer: d

4. Participants hear a list of 30 words and are then asked to recall the words. The participants are particularly accurate in their recall of the first few words they hear, an effect known as:
   a. the priming effect.
   b. the primacy effect.
   c. the recency effect.
   d. the U-shaped response pattern.

   Answer: b

5. In a free-recall procedure, participants hear 25 words, and of these, they are likely to remember 12 to 15. The words recalled are likely to include:
   a. the last 12 or so words on the list.
   b. the first 6 or 7 words in the list, and also the last 6 or 7 in the list.
   c. the first 12 or so words on the list.
   d. words drawn from positions scattered throughout the list.

   Answer: b

6. According to the modal model of memory, words presented early in a list are easier to remember because:
   a. they are still residing in working memory at the time of the test.
   b. participants are particularly alert at the beginning of the list presentation.
   c. the early words receive more of the participants' attention than do the later words.
   d. the words suffer from less interference than do the later words.

   Answer: c

7. The modal model asserts that information processing involves at least two kinds of memory, working memory and long-term memory (LTM). Working memory:
   a. has the same capacity to hold items as LTM.
   b. differs from LTM in how easily one can access the stored items.
   c. uses the same rehearsal mechanisms as LTM.
   d. has no discernible effect on functioning outside of the laboratory.

   Answer: b

8. Many studies of list learning yield a U-shaped "serial-position curve." In these studies:
   a. primacy is not affected by presentation rate.
   b. recency is affected by tasks interpolated between encoding and retrieval.
   c. confusion errors from the beginning of the list tend to be phonological in nature, while errors at the end of the list tend to be semantically based.
   d. recency is observed only if participants are particularly attentive.

   Answer: b

9. An experimenter reads a list of 30 words to a group of participants at the rate of one word per second. This is immediately followed by a free-recall test. A second group of participants hears the same 30 words presented at the faster rate of two words per second. We should expect that the group hearing the *slower* presentation will show:
   a. improved memory performance for the pre-recency portion of the list, but there will be no impact on the recency effect.
   b. improved memory performance for recency effect and diminished performance for the rest of the list.
   c. improved performance for the entire list.
   d. improved memory performance for the words at the list's end but there will be no improvement for the words earlier in the list.

   Answer: a

10. A sudden, loud noise often has the impact of distracting participants long enough to clear the contents of working memory. Imagine that participants hear a list of 20 different fruits, followed by an unexpected loud noise. The effect of noise will be:
    a. a diminished primacy effect but no impact on how well the other words in the list are remembered.
    b. diminished performance for the entire list.
    c. a diminished recency effect and a diminished primacy effect but no impact on how well the other words on the list are remembered.
    d. a diminished recency effect but no impact on how well the other words in the list are remembered.

    Answer: d

11. In list-learning experiments, participants' performance in the prerecency portion of the curve will be improved by:
    a. employing more common, familiar words.
    b. presenting the list of words more quickly.
    c. employing a longer list of words.
    d. distracting participants for a moment just after the list's end.

    Answer: a

12. If asked to recall as many U.S. presidents as possible, participants are likely to recall the first few presidents and also the few most recent presidents. This serial-position effect indicates that:
    a. when participants try to recall the names, they begin by reporting those items that are currently in working memory.
    b. the standard account of recency—in terms of ready access to working memory's contents—cannot explain all recency effects.
    c. all the names recalled had been heard recently by the participants.
    d. the modal model of memory is wrong.

    Answer: b

13. Researchers have distinguished between the "standard" recency effect and a "long-term" recency effect. The former effect is evident in studies of list learning; the latter is evident in studies such as the one in which participants are asked to remember the names of all the U.S. presidents. The data indicate that:
    a. both effects share the same mechanism, namely, availability in working memory.
    b. the standard recency effect reflects working memory function; the long-term recency effect depends on other mechanisms.
    c. both effects reflect the difficulty of retrieval from long-term memory.
    d. the long-term recency effect cannot be documented with laboratory learning.

    Answer: b

14. In demonstrations of the "long-term" recency effect, it appears that:
    a. recent items are recalled directly from working memory.
    b. items heard early in a list can show a recency effect just like items heard later in the list.
    c. recent items are distinctive because they are recent, and their distinctiveness renders them more memorable.
    d. the recency effect depends on working memory, but the primacy effect does not.

    Answer: c

15. Early estimates of working memory's capacity relied on the so-called digit-span task. The data indicate working memory's capacity to be:
    a. 10 to 14 items.
    b. 2 or 3 items.
    c. around 20 items.
    d. around 7 items.

    Answer: d

16. A participant is asked to recall a series of numbers, and the participants chooses to think about the numbers as though they were years (e.g., "1, 9, 9, 7" becomes "the year I turned 16"). The participant is placing more information into the memory unit known as a(n):
    a. sentence.
    b. chunk.
    c. image.
    d. package.

    Answer: b

17. Participants read a series of letters and then, a moment later, are asked to write down the letters they have just seen. If the letter series contains 8 to 10 letters, some errors may occur. The errors are likely to involve:
    a. letters that sound like the letters they have just seen (e.g., recalling S when F was shown).
    b. letters that look like the letters they have just seen (e.g., recalling E when F was shown).
    c. errors with letters from the middle of the alphabet but fewer errors from the beginning and end of the alphabet.
    d. errors with no systematic pattern, probably reflecting each participant's own associations to the various letters.

    Answer: a

18. Phonological confusions are common in working memory, reflecting the fact that:
    a. participants often fail to hear material when it is first presented.
    b. working memory's central executive function is most effective when employing verbal representations, so it tends to rely on these representations.
    c. working memory's performance is often disrupted by verbal associations to the target materials.
    d. the articulatory rehearsal loop is often used and relies on some of the same pathways as ordinary speaking and hearing.

    Answer: d

19. In English, the numerals from one to ten, with the exception of seven, all have one-syllable names. Imagine that we found a language, though, in which the numbers all had two- or three-syllable names. If we test the digit spans of participants who speak this other language and compare them with those of English-speaking participants, we would anticipate:
    a. a greater number of memory chunks.
    b. a slightly smaller digit span.
    c. more effective rehearsal.
    d. a stronger primacy effect.

    Answer: b

20. Participants' tendency to make phonological errors in working-memory tasks probably reflects their reliance on working memory's:
    a. central executive.
    b. visuospatial buffer.
    c. iconic storage.
    d. articulatory rehearsal loop.

    Answer: d

21. Within working memory, the "lower level assistants":
    a. can take over some of the lower-level analyses ordinarily performed by the central executive.
    b. can provide verbal, but not visual, analysis of the memory items.
    c. provide short-term storage of items likely to be needed shortly by the central executive.
    d. preserve the items to be remembered in their initial sensory form (e.g., visual stimuli are preserved as visual images).

    Answer: c

22. Current theory suggests that the central executive may be:
    a. a homunculus, sitting in the brain and directing the lower level assistants to perform various tasks.
    b. another name for various task-general mental resources.
    c. merely another lower level assistant.
    d. a kind of guidebook for how to "run program" in the brain.

    Answer: b

23. A patient with frontal lobe damage is given a task in which he must change his response when he encounters a new stimulus. The patient understands the directions and knows that the stimulus has changed, but continues to make an old response. This patient is:
    a. probably unable to remember what the new response is supposed to be, because frontal lobe damage is associated with working memory problems.
    b. trying to be difficult, because frontal lobe damage leads to negative personality changes.
    c. perseverating.
    d. unable to learn the relationship between the stimulus and the response.

    Answer: c

24. Participants are asked to perform a series of mental tasks while saying "tah, tah, tah" over and over out loud. This manipulation:
    a. will disrupt articulatory rehearsal but will have little effect on the central executive.
    b. will slow down participants' responses but will have no effect on the mental processes themselves.
    c. will distract the central executive, thereby interfering with any task requiring the executive.
    d. will have no impact on participants' performances.

    Answer: a

25. An experimenter measures a participant's digit span. The experimenter then measures the participant's span again, this time requiring the participant to say "tah, tah, tah" over and over out loud while being tested. In the second condition, we expect:
    a. the same digit span as in the first condition.
    b. a slightly larger digit span but fewer phonological confusions.
    c. a diminished digit span.
    d. the same digit span but with a larger word-length effect.

    Answer: c

26. For most recall tests, transfer of items into long-term storage is best facilitated by:
    a. maintenance rehearsal.
    b. elaborative rehearsal.
    c. recency rehearsal.
    d. rote rehearsal.

    Answer: b

27. The strategy of "maintenance rehearsal" involves:
    a. repetition of items to be remembered and simultaneous consideration of the items' meaning.
    b. a focus on the associations between the items to be remembered and other thoughts and ideas.
    c. paying attention to the sequence of items, independent of their meaning.
    d. repetition of the items to be remembered with little attention paid to what the items mean.

    Answer: d

28. Data indicate that, all things equal, recall performance will be best if materials are encoded with:
    a. shallow processing.
    b. intermediate processing.
    c. deep processing.
    d. sensory processing.

    Answer: c

29. Which of the following exemplifies the memory effects of maintenance (or "item-specific") rehearsal?
    a. Irv is unable to describe the appearance of his wristwatch even though he has owned it for years and looks at it many times each day.
    b. Mary is unable to recall the name of her first-grade teacher.
    c. Tony is unable to remember his high school algebra even though he did well in his algebra courses.

   d. Samantha has managed, with some effort, to learn the names of all of her classmates.

Answer: a

30. Participants in an experiment were asked to keep track of the most recent word they had heard that started with a G. Therefore, participants should report "gravy" after hearing the sequence "girl, grump, hat, scissors, whistle, pen, radio, bed, foot, glass, lantern, gravy." Later, participants are asked to report back *all* the "g-words" they had heard. In this situation, we would expect:
   a. good recollection of all the words because participants were able to concentrate their attention on the task and rehearsed only one word at a time.
   b. poor recollection of all the g-words because the situation invites maintenance rehearsal.
   c. good recollection of "grump," since this word was in the participants' thoughts for a long time (while they were waiting for "glass").
   d. poor recollection of the early words in the list but good recollection of words in the middle of the list.

Answer: b

31. Week after week, Solomon watched his favorite TV show. He never planned to memorize the characters' names, and he never took any steps to memorize the names. Nonetheless, he soon knew all of the characters' names. This sort of learning is called:
   a. elaborative.
   b. intentional.
   c. accidental.
   d. incidental.

Answer: d

32. Which of the following is an example of a question that leads to deep processing?
   a. "What is the meaning of the word 'tantalizing'?"
   b. "Are there more vowels or more consonants in the word 'brain'?"
   c. "Can you think of a word that rhymes with 'elephant'?"
   d. "How many syllables are there in the word 'convenient'?"

Answer: a

33. The intention to learn new material:
   a. leads participants to focus on the meaning of the material to be learned.
   b. has no impact on participants' actual learning.

   c. leads participants to employ maintenance rehearsal.

   d. leads participants to approach the material in the fashion they think best for memorization.

Answer: d

34. Which of the following groups is most likely to remember the material they are studying?

   a. Group 1 intends to memorize a series of words and, while studying, repeats the words mechanically over and over.

   b. Group 2 intends to memorize a series of words and, while studying, pays attention to the exact appearance of the words.

   c. Group 3 has no intention to memorize the words and searches the list for spelling errors.

   d. Group 4 has no intention to memorize the words and attempts to determine how the words are related to one another.

Answer: d

35. If a participant is asked to remember some previously experienced event, the relevant memory must be accessed via:

   a. deep processing.

   b. elaborative processing.

   c. a retrieval path.

   d. the memory index.

Answer: c

36. A participant is trying to memorize the word "parade." To help herself, the participant thinks about the word within a complicated sentence: "From their 3rd-floor apartment, they had a great view of all the bands, the cowboys, and the floats in the Thanksgiving parade." This learning strategy will produce:

   a. fine memory performance but similar performance could be achieved with simpler sentences as long as they require the participants to think about the meaning of the term.

   b. poor memory performance because the complicated sentence draws attention away from the target word.

   c. excellent memory performance because the sentence involves a great deal of maintenance rehearsal.

   d. excellent memory performance because the strategy requires attention to meaning and provides many memory connections.

Answer: d

37. In general, any technique designed to improve memory is referred to as:

   a. a mnemonic strategy.

   b. the method of loci.

c. the method of repetition.

d. memory rehearsal.

Answer: a

38. In a "peg-word system," participants help themselves memorize a group of items by:

    a. forming an elaborate sentence about each of the items to be remembered.

    b. associating each item with some part of an already memorized framework, or skeleton.

    c. naming the items to themselves over and over.

    d. placing each item in its appropriate semantic category.

Answer: b

39. Although mnemonics can be helpful for remembering a small number of specific items (like a grocery list), they may not be a great overall learning strategy. All of the following are potential problems *except*:

    a. the limited connections provided by mnemonics make it more difficult to retrieve information from new directions.

    b. mnemonics make it difficult to see new connections between various elements of previously learned material.

    c. mnemonics are particularly difficult to remember when specific information is being tested.

    d. mnemonics tend to isolate the newly learned material, making it more difficult to integrate the material with other things known.

Answer: c

40. One group of participants is asked to memorize the list: "table, lettuce, pen, truck, shoe, court, snow, nose, school, hammer." A second group is asked to memorize the list: "grape, strawberry, banana, apple, blueberry, history, biology, linguistics, physics, sociology." We should predict that performance will be better in:

    a. the second condition, with participants displaying a "clustering" pattern.

    b. the first condition, with participants suffering from semantic confusions.

    c. the second condition because of the memory advantage for familiar words.

    d. the first condition because of the advantage, in working memory, for shorter words.

Answer: a

41. Participants in recall experiments often show an effect called "clustering." This refers to:

    a. participants' difficulty in recalling words that refer to categories.

    b. participants' tendency to categorize items to be remembered, and then to report back the items category by category.

c. the improvement in participants' performance if they are explicitly encouraged to categorize the items to be remembered.

d. participants' inclination to rehearse the items category by category even if they must report the words back in an uncategorized fashion.

Answer: b

42. A participant learns a list of words on Monday and is then asked to recall the words on Tuesday, Wednesday, and again Thursday. An examination of Tuesday's and Wednesday's recall indicates that the words were recalled in almost the same sequence in the two separate tests. Therefore, we should predict:

a. relatively good performance in Thursday's test because the participant seems to have imposed a firm organization on the materials.

b. poorer performance on Thursday's test because of the participant's rigid approach to the materials.

c. poor memory performance on Thursday because the participant shows no evidence of flexibility in her choice of retrieval paths.

d. excellent performance on Thursday because the rigidity of the recall sequence indicates that the participant has successfully used the method of loci to memorize the list.

Answer: a

43. A student wishes to memorize an essay so that she will be able to recall the essay's content later on. Which of the following is likely to be *least helpful* to the student?

a. making certain that she understands the argument contained within the essay

b. thinking about why the essay is organized in the way that it is

c. reading the essay aloud over and over

d. trying to construct a paraphrase of the essay's content

Answer: c

44. A physician has just read an article about a recently invented drug. Which of the following is *least important* in determining whether the physician will remember the article later on?

a. The physician read the article carefully to determine if it was persuasive.

b. The physician realized how suggestions within the article could be integrated with other things she already knew.

c. The physician expected to need the information later on and therefore employed a rote memorization strategy that she believed had helped her memorize material in the past.

d. The physician quickly saw that the new drug might have multiple uses, so she thought about several circumstances in which she might use the drug.

Answer: c

CHAPTER 6

Interconnections between Acquisition and Retrieval

1. Which of the following is an example of a recognition test?
   a. "Which of these individuals is the person you saw at the party?"
   b. "Describe how you spent New Year's Eve in 1994."
   c. "What is the formula needed for computing the area of a circle?"
   d. "What political event does this song remind you of?"

   Answer: a

2. A participant is asked, "Tell me as much as you can about last week's party." This is a memory test dependent on:
   a. recognition.
   b. recall.
   c. generic memory.
   d. implicit memory.

   Answer: b

3. An investigator asks, "Can you remember what happened last Tuesday at noon while you were sitting in the back room of Jane's Restaurant?" This is an example of a question relying on:
   a. recognition.
   b. implicit memory.
   c. procedural memory.
   d. recall.

   Answer: d

4. Jerry, a lawyer, has read about a case (*Jones v. Arizona*) that he thinks will help a client of his. Jerry wants to make sure that he remembers to discuss the case with his client, and that he brings up the case in his opening statements in court. His best bet is likely to be:
   a. repeating to himself, over and over, "don't forget *Jones v. Arizona*."

b. to use a mnemonic device, like peg-word system, and hope that his client and the judge don't think him odd for saying "one is a bun . . ." in court.

c. to build multiple retrieval paths between the new case and the situations in which he wishes to use it.

d. to put the case book containing *Jones v. Arizona* on his desk with all of the other books, and hope he finds it when his client arrives and when he writes his opening statements.

Answer: c

5. A researcher hypothesizes that high doses of caffeine can produce state-dependent learning. To confirm this hypothesis, the researcher would need to show that:

a. participants learn more effectively if they drink several cups of coffee before studying the material to be learned.

b. participants recall performance is improved if they are tested soon after drinking several cups of coffee.

c. participants who drink a lot of coffee are, in general, likely to do better on memory tests.

d. if participants studied the material after drinking a great deal of coffee, they will have an easier time remembering the material if they drink a great deal of coffee just before taking the memory test.

Answer: d

6. Which of the following observations sounds most likely to be an illustration of state-dependent learning?

a. "I haven't been to Athens in years, but I still remember all the great times I had there!"

b. "Mike has told me his phone number over and over, but somehow I can't get it into my head."

c. "Last month I went to my twentieth high school reunion. I saw people I hadn't thought about for years, but the moment I saw them I was reminded of the things we'd done together twenty years earlier."

d. "I spent hours studying in the library last night preparing for my history midterm. And it really paid off; I did a great job on the exam."

Answer: c

7. Because of the effects of state-dependent learning, students might find it wise to:

a. use mnemonic devices as a study aid.

b. study only when they are entirely sober.

c. focus on their instructors' intended meaning rather than on the instructors' exact words.

    d. prepare for their examinations under conditions similar to the test conditions.

Answer: d

8. A participant is asked, "In the list of words I showed you earlier, was there a word that rhymed with lake"? The participant is likely to be well prepared for this sort of memory test if:
    a. the participant used maintenance rehearsal when trying to memorize the words.
    b. the participant paid attention to the sounds of the words when trying to memorize them.
    c. the participant paid attention to the appearance of the words when trying to memorize them.
    d. the participant relied on perceptual fluency when studying the words.

Answer: b

9. Participants are asked to memorize a list of words. In addition to the words themselves, participants will remember some aspects of the context in which the words appeared. This tendency to remember a stimulus within its context is referred to as:
    a. background learning.
    b. multiple encoding.
    c. implicit memory.
    d. encoding specificity.

Answer: d

10. Participants are asked to memorize a list of words. The eighth word on the list is "inches," the ninth word is "meters," and the tenth is "feet." In which of the following would the participants be most likely to remember the previous exposure to "feet"?
    a. In the memory test, the fourth word tested is "yards," and the fifth is "feet."
    b. In the memory test, the fourth word tested is "heat," and the fifth is "feet."
    c. In the memory test, the fourth word tested is "hands," and the fifth is "feet.'
    d. In the memory test, the fourth word tested is "fight," and the fifth is "feet."

Answer: a

11. A participant is asked to memorize a series of word pairs, including the pair: "heavy-light." The participant is asked later if any of the following words had been included in the list memorized earlier: "lamp," "candle," "spark," "light." The participant denies having seen any of these words recently. This is probably because:

    a. the learning context does not provide adequate support for perceptual encoding.

    b. the learning context does relatively little to encourage deep processing.

    c. what was memorized was the idea of "light" as a description of weight, not "light" as illumination.

    d. the learning context led the participant to think in terms of opposites, while the test context led the participant to think in terms of semantic associates.

Answer: c

12. Which of the following seems the best illustration of encoding specificity?
    a. Susan is terrible at learning general arguments, although she is excellent at learning more specific claims.
    b. Susan has learned the principles covered in her psychology class, but she has difficulty remembering the principles in the context of her day-to-day life.
    c. Susan easily learns material that is meaningful but cannot learn material that is abstract.
    d. Susan quickly masters new material if she knows some related information, but she has trouble learning things if the domain is new to her.

Answer: b

13. Herbert says, "I can't figure out where I've seen that person before, but I know that I have seen her before!" Herbert:
    a. has an episodic memory for the face, but no generic memory for the face.
    b. has a sense of familiarity, but no source memory.
    c. would perform well on a recall test, but not on a recognition test.
    d. seems to have formed inter-item associations when he last encountered the face.

Answer: b

14. Familiarity (as opposed to source memory):
    a. is essential for adequate performance on a recall test.
    b. is established by "relational" or "elaborative" rehearsal.
    c. is promoted by deep processing.
    d. provides one of the important sources for recognition.

Answer: d

15. The phenomenon of source confusion reflects the fact that:
    a. we are often better at recognizing that something is familiar than we are at determining why it is familiar.
    b. source memories seem to last longer than the sense of familiarity.

    c. recognition testing is more difficult than recall testing.

    d. we are best able to recall material if we are in a mental state similar to the one we were in during learning.

Answer: a

16. One group of participants is shown a series of words ("down, triangle, thunder") and is then asked to read the words aloud. A second group of participants is shown a series of definitions ("opposite of up, shape with three sides, sound that follows lightening") and is asked to say aloud what the defined words are. If we later test participants' memories for the words, we expect better performance for the *first* group if the test involves:

    a. tachistoscopic recognition of the words.

    b. recall of the words.

    c. cued recall of the words.

    d. a standard recognition test for the words.

Answer: a

17. In tachistoscopic testing, implicit memory seems to be maximized by:

    a. a previous experience of thinking about the meaning of the words being tested.

    b. a recent experience of actually seeing the words being tested.

    c. state-dependent learning for the words being tested.

    d. deep processing.

Answer: b

18. Which of the following tasks is least appropriate as a means of testing implicit memory?

    a. lexical decision

    b. word-stem completion

    c. cued recall

    d. repetition priming in tachistoscopic recognition

Answer: c

19. Abigail saw the stimulus "_l_i_a_o_." She filled in the blanks and figured out that the completed word was "alligator." Abigail's discovery is the sort of discovery needed for the task called:

    a. lexical decision.

    b. word-fragment completion.

    c. semantic priming.

    d. explicit memory.

Answer: b

20. Which of the following is *not* true for explicit memory?
    a. Explicit memory is typically revealed as a priming effect.
    b. Explicit memory is usually assessed by direct, rather than indirect, testing.
    c. Explicit memory is generally accompanied by a sense that one is remembering a specific prior episode.
    d. Explicit memory is often tested by recall testing or by a standard recognition test.

    Answer: a

21. Which of the following is *not* likely to be an influence of implicit memory?
    a. Participants know they have encountered the stimulus recently but can't recall the details of the encounter.
    b. Participants have a preference for the stimulus in comparison to other, new stimuli.
    c. Participants believe they encountered a stimulus long ago even though the encounter was recent.
    d. Participants remember the circumstances in which they first met a stimulus.

    Answer: d

22. Which of the following sounds most like an example of the influence of implicit memory?
    a. "Alexander was taking a true-false test. He didn't know the answer to #12, so he skipped the item."
    b. "Bill couldn't remember the answer for the question, but he did his best to reconstruct what the answer might be."
    c. "Not only did Dave remember the answer, he also remembered where the answer appeared on the textbook page."
    d. "Marcus was taking a multiple-choice test. He was having a hard time with #17, but option "d" for that question seemed familiar, so he decided that "d" must be the correct answer."

    Answer: d

23. Because of implicit memory's influence, participants:
    a. judge unfamiliar sentences to be more believable.
    b. judge familiar sentences to be more believable.
    c. judge familiar sentences to be more believable, but only if they heard the sentence from a trustworthy source.
    d. judge unfamiliar sentences to be more believable, but only if they have forgotten the source of the familiar sentences.

    Answer: b

24. Participants listen to a series of sentences played against a background of noise. Some of the sentences are identical to sentences heard earlier (without the noise), but other sentences heard in the noise are new. In this setting, participants will:

a. perceive the unfamiliar sentences heard with the noise as louder than the familiar sentences.

b. perceive the unfamiliar sentences as being clearer than the familiar sentences.

c. perceive the noise as being less loud when it accompanies the familiar sentences.

d. perceive no difference between the unfamiliar and the familiar sentences.

Answer: c

25. In many circumstances, participants correctly recognize that a stimulus is familiar, but they are mistaken in their beliefs about where and when they encountered the stimulus. This error is referred to as:

a. source confusion.

b. origin error.

c. amnesia.

d. false identification.

Answer: a

26. When a person experiences familiarity but no accompanying source memory, the effects can be far-reaching, and could include:

a. the person believing that a familiar statement is true, even though they cannot remember where they heard it.

b. the person inaccurately accusing someone of a crime, merely because the person seems familiar.

c. the person's aesthetic preferences changing in favor of the familiar information.

d. any of the above.

Answer: d

27. Cindy and Linda are both eyewitnesses to a bank robbery. At the police station, they each select Mike from a police lineup, and say, "He's the thief!" It turns out, though, that Mike has been a customer at the store at which Cindy works. Linda has never seen Mike before. With this background:

a. Cindy's identification is more valuable to the police because she has an advantage of familiarity and context.

b. Both identifications are likely to be accurate because face recognition draws on specialized mechanisms that work effectively with both familiar and unfamiliar faces.

c. Cindy's identification is more valuable to the police because her recognition of Mike will be more fluent than Linda's, thanks to the previous encounters.

d. Linda's identification is more valuable to the police because Cindy may have been misled by the fact that Mike seemed familiar based on her other encounters with him.

Answer: d

28. If you perceive a stimulus and then later perceive the same stimulus again, you are likely to perceive the stimulus more quickly and more easily the second time. This benefit can be described as:
    a. a state-dependent memory.
    b. an explicit memory.
    c. an increase in processing fluency.
    d. a recognition memory.

    Answer: c

29. Participants are asked to read a series of unrelated words out loud. According to the hypothesis described in the text, this experience will help the participants:
    a. if they now try to perceive words synonymous with the words contained on the list.
    b. the next time they try to perceive these same words.
    c. the next time they try to remember the concepts associated with the words on the list.
    d. if they try to recall a series of words related to the words on the list.

    Answer: b

30. In part 1 of an experiment, a participant is given a series of definitions, and for each definition the participant's task is to say out loud the word being defined. One of the definitions is "soft metal of a yellowish color often used for electric wires." The participant responds, "copper." This experience will have the greatest influence on which of the following tasks?
    a. a tachistoscopic recognition test that includes "copper" as one of the test items
    b. a general knowledge task that includes the item, "What element makes up 10 percent of so-called yellow gold?"
    c. a word fragment completion task that includes the item, "_o_p_r."
    d. a tachistoscopic recognition test that includes the nonword "cupper" as one of the stimuli.

    Answer: b

31. In a test of tachistoscopic recognition, a researcher finds no effect of repetition priming. Which of the following is a plausible explanation for this?
    a. The researcher forgot to tell the participants that some of the test words had been recently encountered.
    b. Some of the test words were high in frequency, but others were quite low in frequency.
    c. When the priming words were first presented, participants failed to pay attention to the meaning of the words.
    d. The priming words were presented to participants via a tape-recorded list, providing only an auditory input.

    Answer: d

32. In phase I of an experiment, participants are asked to complete a list of word fragments, including "_L_P_A_T". On which of the following phase II (tachistoscopically presented) items are they most likely to respond quickly because of priming effects?
    a. only "_L_P_A_T", because *perceptual* priming is not easily transferred to other stimuli.
    b. "_L_P_A_T" or "E_E_H_N_," because the same word underlies both fragments.
    c. "_L_P_A_T", "Z_B_A" or "L_O_" because the category "African animals" will be primed after the initial exposure to "_L_P_A_T".
    d. all word fragments, because of their recent practice in word-stem completion.

    Answer: a

33. One important difference between *perceptual* fluency and *conceptual* fluency is:
    a. only perceptual fluency leads to priming effects.
    b. only conceptual fluency leads to priming effects.
    c. perceptual fluency is more dependent on stimulus format.
    d. conceptual fluency is more dependent on stimulus format.

    Answer: c

34. A friend of yours has recently grown a beard. When you encounter him, you realize at once that something about his face has changed, but you are not certain what has changed. We can conclude from this that:
    a. you detected the decrease in fluency in your recognition of your friend's face.
    b. your memory of your friend's face is influenced by state-dependent learning.
    c. you are displaying an instance of source amnesia.
    d. you are being influenced by the fact that there are fewer men with beards than men without beards.

    Answer: a

35. There is some disagreement among researchers concerning how memories should be classified. There is, however, considerable overlap between the category identified as "implicit" and the category identified as:
    a. "conscious."
    b. "direct."
    c. "procedural."
    d. "conceptual."

    Answer: c

36. Peter knows how to swing a tennis racket, and he bends his wrist at exactly the right moment. Nevertheless, Peter is not aware that he is bending his wrist. In this case, Peter has _____ knowledge about wrist bending, but no _____ knowledge.
    a. implicit; indirect
    b. procedural; declarative
    c. generic; episodic
    d. procedural; implicit

    Answer: b

37. A process-pure laboratory task is one in which:
    a. the researcher can be sure that her results are reflective only of the process she is studying.
    b. the procedure runs smoothly, without any major experimenter errors.
    c. the procedure is deemed ethically unproblematic by the relevant Human Subjects Committee.
    d. the researcher can be sure that the data will support her hypothesis.

    Answer: a

38. If more than one process is contributing to performance on a task, and thus clouding interpretation of the results from that task, the task is said to be:
    a. insensitive.
    b. unreliable.
    c. process pure.
    d. process impure.

    Answer: d

39. Mark suffered a blow to the head some weeks ago, causing retrograde amnesia. Which of the following is Mark least likely to remember?
    a. facts that he learned in the month after his injury, including the layout of the hospital in which he received care
    b. events of his childhood
    c. specific episodes in the two weeks following his injury
    d. events that took place just prior to his injury

    Answer: d

40. The famous patient H.M. is unable to remember events he experienced after his brain surgery. The surgery apparently produced:
    a. repression.
    b. anterograde amnesia.
    c. retrograde amnesia.
    d. infantile amnesia.

    Answer: b

41. Theodore has suffered from Korsakoff's amnesia for the last decade. Theodore is least likely to do which of the following:
    a. accurately recall events from early childhood
    b. hold a coherent conversation lasting many minutes
    c. recall events that occurred last month
    d. recognize people he met 18 years ago

    Answer: c

42. In a classic demonstration, Claparède showed that:
    a. the behavior of a Korsakoff's amnesia patient can be changed by a recent event even though the patient shows no signs of remembering that event.
    b. Korsakoff's amnesics show more severe retrograde amnesia than anterograde.
    c. Korsakoff's amnesics show an extraordinary ability to recall their plans for the future even though they cannot remember their own pasts.
    d. the behavior of a Korsakoff's amnesia patient is less well organized than clinicians have theorized.

    Answer: a

43. Current evidence indicates that patients suffering from Korsakoff's amnesia:
    a. show greater disruption in implicit memory than in explicit memory.
    b. suffer from disruption in both implicit and explicit memory.
    c. show intact implicit memory with perceptual cues, but disrupted implicit memory with conceptual cues.
    d. have preserved implicit memory despite severe disruption in explicit memory.

    Answer: d

CHAPTER 7 | Memory Errors, Memory Gaps

1. In a study by Brewer and Treyens, participants waited in an experimenter's office for the experiment to begin. After they left the room, they learned that the study was about their memory for that office. This study demonstrated:
   a. that college students do not know what professor's offices typically contain.
   b. that people make assumptions using schemata to fill in gaps in their memory.
   c. that college students' memories are much worse than the memories of other groups in society.
   d. that people tend to notice only those items in the environment that most fit with their expectations.

   Answer: b

2. We tend not to notice gaps in our own perception because:
   a. those gaps are very few and far between.
   b. we know that we can carefully review our memories later in order to fill in those gaps.
   c. those gaps are irrelevant.
   d. those gaps are always located at sites we are not paying attention to.

   Answer: d

3. A broader understanding of a situation or story:
   a. always improves memory by providing context.
   b. always hurts memory by confusing new events with old information.
   c. both improves and hurts, for the above reasons.
   d. does little to affect the quality or quantity of memory.

   Answer: c

4. Participants in one experiment read a series of sentences, some of which have complicated syntax and some of which are phrased in a simple manner. The data indicated that:

a. participants had to spend much effort to understand the complicated sentences, and their attention to wording led them to remember the exact phrasing of the sentences.
b. participants had to spend much effort to understand the complicated sentences, and the effort distracted them, leading to poor memory for the phrasing of the sentences.
c. participants remembered the gist of all the sentences, both complicated and simple, but not the actual phrasing of the sentences.
d. participants' memory for actual phrasing was accurate in a recall test but less accurate in recognition testing.

Answer: a

5. Some of the sentences one hears are phrased in a particularly striking fashion—perhaps the sentence is quite rude or especially witty. For sentences such as these:
   a. we pay attention to surface form rather than to meaning, leading to poor memory for the sentences.
   b. we are likely to remember the exact phrasing as well as the sentence's content.
   c. we remember only the gist of the sentence, as we do for virtually all sentences.
   d. schematic knowledge contributes less to our understanding of such sentences than it does for ordinary sentences.

Answer: b

6. Liz is trying to remember what she read in a text chapter, but she inadvertently mixes into her recall her own assumptions about the material covered in the chapter. This is an example of:
   a. omission errors.
   b. recognition failures.
   c. intrusion errors.
   d. misses.

Answer: c

7. Memory schemas, or "schemata," serve as representations of our:
   a. innate knowledge.
   b. specific knowledge.
   c. generic knowledge.
   d. episodic knowledge.

Answer: c

8. Which of the following is *least* likely to be included within a kitchen schema?
   a. "Kitchens almost always contain a refrigerator."
   b. "Kitchens sometimes contain a coffeemaker."

    c. "A kitchen usually contains a sink."

    d. "My mother's kitchen contains a microwave oven."

Answer: d

9. Which of the following claims is false?
    a. Inattention during an event leads to gaps in the memory record, but the gaps can often be filled by relying on schema-based knowledge.
    b. According to schema-based knowledge, if certain aspects of an event are highly predictable, you are less likely to pay attention to these aspects.
    c. Schema-based knowledge is particularly helpful in allowing us to reconstruct unusual or atypical aspects of an event.
    d. Schema-based knowledge helps us to identify those aspects of an event that are unusual or particularly interesting, and this guides attention toward those aspects.

Answer: c

10. Merlin learned a magic spell on January 10. He then used that spell (to scare away a dragon) on January 18. The eight-day period between these dates is called the:
    a. retention interval.
    b. retrieval path.
    c. interference period.
    d. memory span.

Answer: a

11. Which of the following does not name a hypothesis concerning why we forget?
    a. decay
    b. hypermnesia
    c. interference
    d. retrieval failure

Answer: b

12. Which of the following refers to the hypothesis that memories fade or erode with the passage of time?
    a. interference
    b. decay
    c. repression
    d. retention interval

Answer: b

13. Evidence suggests that decay:
    a. accounts for the vast majority of forgetting.
    b. probably explains far less forgetting than interference or retrieval failure.

c. in combination with repression, explains virtually all of forgetting.

d. is a well-supported phenomenon.

Answer: b

14. A great deal of forgetting may reflect a (perhaps temporary) inability to locate the target information in storage. This sort of forgetting is called:
    a. repression.
    b. retrieval failure.
    c. interference.
    d. state dependency.

Answer: b

15. Baddeley and Hitch asked rugby players to remember all of the rugby games they had played over the course of a single season. According to their data, what is the most important factor in determining whether the players will remember a particular game?
    a. how many other games has the player been in since the target game
    b. how much time has passed since the target game
    c. whether or not the player was satisfied with his performance in the target game
    d. whether the game took place during the week or on a weekend

Answer: a

16. Will has been to the zoo many times, usually with his family but also once on a school field trip. When Will tries to remember the field trip, his recollection is:
    a. likely to include elements imported from memories of other zoo trips.
    b. unlikely to be influenced by schematic knowledge.
    c. likely to be highly accurate in its details.
    d. unlikely to include much perceptual information.

Answer: a

17. Half of the participants in an experiment learned a list of new material, slept for 8 hours, and were then tested for the material they had learned. The remaining participants learned the same material, spent the next 8 hours awake, and were then tested. Based on other research in this area, we should expect that:
    a. the group that slept will remember less because they will have less opportunity for post event rehearsal.
    b. the two groups will be similar in their memory performance because the retention interval was the same for both.
    c. the group that slept will remember more because they have less opportunity for memory decay.

d. the group that slept will remember more because they will experience less retroactive interference.

Answer: d

18. All of the following are true of John Dean's memories of his conversations with Richard Nixon, *except*:
    a. they were in general correct with respect to gist, but less accurate in detail.
    b. the memory errors are hard to understand with reference to current theories of remembering.
    c. some portions of conversations were remembered accurately, but in the wrong context.
    d. individual episodes tended to blur together.

Answer: b

19. Participants viewed a series of slides depicting an automobile accident. Immediately afterward, half of the participants were asked, "How fast were the cars going when they hit each other?" Other participants were asked, "How fast were the cars going when they smashed into each other?" One week later, all participants were asked more questions about the slides, including whether they had seen any broken glass in the slides. A comparison of the two groups of participants is likely to show that:
    a. participants who were asked the "smashed" question gave higher estimates of speed and were more likely to remember seeing broken glass.
    b. the groups gave similar estimates of speed, but the "smashed" group was more likely to remember seeing broken glass.
    c. participants who were asked the "smashed" question gave higher estimates of speed, but the groups gave similar responses to the "glass" question.
    d. the minor contrast in how the groups were questioned had no effect on participants' memories.

Answer: a

20. Misleading questions asked after participants have witnessed an event:
    a. influence participants' immediate reports of the event, as well as their recall of the event if they try to remember it sometime later.
    b. influence participants' immediate reports of the event but have little impact on longer-term retention.
    c. influence participants' longer-term retention of the event, but not their reports of the event immediately after witnessing it.
    d. influence participants' reports of an event only if the questions plant false ideas that are compatible with the participants' perceptions.

Answer: a

21. Michael and Maria both witnessed an auto accident. Maria remembers watching the car race past a stop sign, but she hears Michael as he reports

to the police that the car raced past a yield sign. Later, Maria is likely to recall that she saw:

a. a stop sign, with her memory strengthened by the experience of hearing Michael's flawed report.

b. a yield sign, incorporating Michael's report into her own recollection.

c. a yield sign, but she will have low confidence in this recollection.

d. no sign at all.

Answer: b

22. By using leading questions and misinformation, researchers have been able:

a. to shape how a real event is remembered, but they have been unable to lead participants into remembering an event that never took place.

b. to shape how participants remember the details of an event, but they have been unable to change how participants remember the sequence of actions in the event.

c. to shape how participants remember the objects present as an event unfolded, but they have been unable to influence how participants remember the people who participated in the event.

d. to alter virtually any aspect of participants' memories and have even been able to create memories for entire events that never took place.

Answer: d

23. The "misinformation effect" refers to the fact that false information, presented after a participant has encoded an event, can intrude into the participant's subsequent recall of the event. This "planting" of memories.

a. seems restricted to small memory errors.

b. is only possible if done by an authority figure.

c. seems possible for remembered actions but not remembered objects.

d. is not restricted to laboratory procedures.

Answer: d

24. Which of the following claims about memory accuracy is *false*?

a. Participants' confidence in their false memories is often just as great as their confidence in their accurate recollection.

b. False memories can be demonstrated in gullible participants, as well as in strong-willed participants.

c. When a participant's response is based on a false memory, the response is likely to be given just as quickly as it would be if based on an accurate memory.

d. Participants are sometimes mistaken in their recollection of an event's minor details, but false memories seem not to occur when participants are remembering the broad plot of an event.

Answer: d

25. What are the necessary circumstances to produce false memories in research participants?
    a. It is not possible to produce completely false memories in participants under any circumstances.
    b. It would require trauma too severe to be ethically allowable.
    c. It would require highly suggestible participants and repeated leading questions.
    d. All that is required is a few brief interviews, requests for participants to "try and remember," and reasonably plausible stories.

    Answer: d

26. The creation of false memories in someone:
    a. is possible only with strong and explicit suggestions to them.
    b. is possible only in the presence of trauma.
    c. is possible only with highly suggestible participants.
    d. is possible with just a few brief interviews.

    Answer: d

27. The creation of false memories in someone:
    a. is possible only for small details; gist is remembered accurately.
    b. is possible only for events that took place long ago; recent events are remembered accurately.
    c. is possible only for neutral or unimportant events; memories that are emotional are accurate.
    d. is possible even for the creation of large-scale, entirely false events.

    Answer: d

28. An eyewitness to a crime is quite confident that his memory of the crime is correct. In evaluating the eyewitness's testimony, the jury should note that:
    a. eyewitness memories are incorrect as often as they are correct.
    b. memory confidence is a poor indicator of memory accuracy.
    c. memory confidence is a reliable indicator that memory for the generalities of an event is correct, although memory for detail is unrelated to confidence.
    d. eyewitnesses tend to assert that they are confident only when their memories are reasonably accurate overall.

    Answer: b

29. A number of studies have indicated that the correlation between memory accuracy and memory confidence is near zero. This implies that:
    a. memories recalled with confidence are rarely correct.
    b. memories recalled with little confidence are nonetheless generally accurate.

    c. the confidence with which a memory is recalled tells us little about whether or not the memory is accurate.

    d. the greater the confidence placed in a memory, the more uncertain we should be about that memory's accuracy.

Answer: c

30. An expert is asked to comment on the confidence-accuracy relationship of an eyewitness's report. The expert will state that:
    a. the higher the witness's confidence, the more likely the memory is accurate.
    b. the lower the witness's confidence, the more likely the memory is accurate.
    c. extremely high confidence is a good indicator of an accurate memory, but more moderate levels of confidence are uninformative.
    d. confidence levels are a poor indicator of the accuracy of recall.

Answer: d

31. Memory errors and distortions can be documented:
    a. only for memory of the exact phrasing of prose material.
    b. only for memory of unfamiliar material.
    c. in recall of texts and the recall of complex events.
    d. only with material that has been reported to participants, not with material that participants have experienced directly.

Answer: c

32. Dmitri witnessed a bank robbery but now seems unable to remember what he saw. To improve Dmitri's recall, a friend hypnotizes him and asks him, while hypnotized, to recall the crime. Research indicates that if questioned while under hypnosis:
    a. Dmitri will give a more elaborate account of the crime than he has on other occasions.
    b. Dmitri will give a more accurate account of the crime than he has on other occasions.
    c. Dmitri will be less vulnerable to the effect of leading questions.
    d. Dmitri will suffer from less retrieval failure.

Answer: a

33. The term "hypermnesia" refers to:
    a. an extreme form of amnesia.
    b. a process in which participants remember more and more, thanks to continued efforts at remembering.
    c. the technique of using hypnosis to recover an otherwise-lost memory.
    d. the ability some people have to recall vast amounts of material.

Answer: b

34. The "cognitive interview" technique has been used to promote remembering by eyewitnesses to crimes and includes all of the following except:
    a. attempts to interpret implicit memories, created by the initial event.
    b. attempts at recounting the event in more than one sequence.
    c. attempts at reporting the event from more than one perspective.
    d. attempts to recreate the environmental or personal context of the event.

    Answer: a

35. An important theme emerging from memory research is that memory connections:
    a. are crucial for recognition but are less important for recall.
    b. improve memory access but have no impact on memory accuracy.
    c. make memories easier to locate but can lead to intrusion errors.
    d. play a role in episodic memory but not in generic memory.

    Answer: c

36. Connections among our various memories do all of the following *except*:
    a. help us to resist source confusion.
    b. serve as retrieval paths.
    c. interweave our various memories, inviting intrusion errors.
    d. link related memories.

    Answer: a

37. Information that is perceived as relevant to the self is better remembered. This is referred to as:
    a. the ego directive.
    b. the autobiographical perspective advantage.
    c. the self-reference effect.
    d. the self-importance law.

    Answer: c

38. In the process of memory consolidation, memories are:
    a. put into the "back of the mind," for self-protection.
    b. intentionally blurred with other memories.
    c. second-guessed in favor of memory schemata already in place.
    d. "cemented into place."

    Answer: d

39. Emotion has multiple effects on the encoding and retrieval of memories. Which of the following is most likely to occur during the recall of everyday emotional events?
    a. amnesia
    b. repression
    c. decreased accuracy in recall

    d. accurate recall of the event's gist, but relatively poor recall of the event's background details

Answer: d

40. Witnesses to a crime often seem to zoom in on some critical detail, and they remember this detail clearly even though they remember little else about the event. This pattern is referred to as:
    a. weapon focus.
    b. encoding specificity.
    c. denial.
    d. dissociation.

Answer: a

41. Studies of "flashbulb memories" indicate that these memories:
    a. are distinctive because of their impressively uniform accuracy.
    b. are distinctive because they preserve an event's gist while recording few of the event's perceptual details.
    c. are more likely to be accurate if the event was consequential for the participant's life.
    d. are particularly likely for surprising, but otherwise unemotional, events.

Answer: c

42. Flashbulb memories are extremely detailed, vivid memories, usually associated with highly emotional events. The accuracy of these memories seems:
    a. best predicted by the consequentiality of the event to participants' lives.
    b. unrelated to any factors researchers have probed so far.
    c. remarkably high, identifying these memories as a special class of episodic recall.
    d. strongly associated with participants' confidence levels, differentiating flashbulbs from other forms of memory.

Answer: a

43. Research on very-long-term remembering indicates that:
    a. memories fade more and more as the years go by.
    b. memories of childhood are retained throughout the life span; later memories, however, are vulnerable to forgetting.
    c. if you learn material well enough to retain it for three or four years, the odds are good that you will continue to remember the material for many more years.
    d. if you learn material before age thirteen or fourteen, you are unlikely to remember the material in later years; material learned at older ages is retained for longer periods.

Answer: c

CHAPTER 8

Associative Theories of
Long-Term Memory

1. Which of the following claims is *false*?
   a. If you think often about the relationship between two ideas, there probably will be a strong association between the nodes representing the ideas.
   b. If you think about an idea from several different perspectives, you are likely to create multiple connections between the nodes representing the idea and other nodes in memory.
   c. Memory associations do not differ much in strength, but there is wide variation in the activation levels of the different memory nodes.
   d. Stronger memory associations serve as more efficient retrieval paths than do weaker associations.

   Answer: c

2. A node's activation level is defined in terms of:
   a. how effective the node will be, when it fires, in triggering neighboring nodes.
   b. the current status of the node, determined by how recently and how frequently inputs have reached the node.
   c. where the node is located within the processing network.
   d. the node's degree of fan.

   Answer: b

3. In predicting the activation level of a particular node, which of the following is the *least* likely to play a role?
   a. recency of firing
   b. frequency of firing
   c. activation levels of connected neighboring regions
   d. location in the brain

   Answer: d

4. In network models, subthreshold activation of a node:
   a. causes that node to fire.
   b. can add together with other subthreshold activation.
   c. has no effect on the node.
   d. influences a node only if the node is already primed.

   Answer: b

5. A node's "response threshold" refers to:
   a. the beginning moments of the node's response.
   b. how strongly the node has to respond in order to influence other nodes.
   c. the level of activation that will cause the node to respond.
   d. the maximum rate at which the node will respond.

   Answer: c

6. In network theorizing, which of the following will *not* cause "priming" of a node?
   a. recent firing of the node
   b. frequent firing of the node
   c. subthreshold activation received from neighboring nodes
   d. an increase in the degree of fan for the node

   Answer: d

7. Once a node is activated, it will serve as a source of further activation, and this activation:
   a. will spread through all the associations radiating from the node.
   b. will spread only to the closest neighboring node.
   c. will inhibit the activities of neighboring nodes.
   d. will direct the person's attention away from the node's contents.

   Answer: a

8. According to the text, hints help us remember because:
   a. nodes representing an effective hint generally have a high degree of fan.
   b. nodes for the hint are likely to be connected to nodes representing the learning context.
   c. the target node receives activation from both the hint's nodes and from other nodes.
   d. the hint's node is likely to be well primed by the context of the memory test.

   Answer: c

9. Participants are better able to remember material learned earlier if they are in the same state at the time of recall that they were in at the time of learning. In network terms, this reflects the fact that nodes for the target materials:

    a. are receiving activation from both the nodes representing the retrieval cues and the nodes representing the participants' state.

    b. are associated only indirectly with the nodes representing the retrieval cues.

    c. have higher response thresholds in some states than in others.

    d. probably have a low degree of fan.

Answer: a

10. In network terms, mnemonics:
    a. exploit strong, already existing connections, allowing new connections to parasitize them.
    b. create multiple connections between old information and new information.
    c. dramatically expand the degree of fan of a particular node.
    d. dramatically reduce the degree of fan of a particular node.

Answer: a

11. Mnemonic devices may be poor choices for study aids, because:
    a. they prevent the creation of connections between nodes.
    b. the mnemonics themselves are often difficult to remember at test-time.
    c. although they strengthen some specific connections, these connections are few in number and involve superficial points.
    d. they weaken previously created associations.

Answer: c

12. In a lexical-decision task, participants:
    a. are shown simple sentences and must decide whether each is true or false.
    b. are shown letter strings and must decide whether or not each is a word.
    c. are shown sequences of numbers and must decide whether or not each conforms to a specific pattern.
    d. are shown word pairs and must decide whether or not the words in the pair are related.

Answer: b

13. A lexical-decision task is generally used to assess:
    a. the degree of fan for the nodes representing the target word.
    b. the holding capacity of a participant's working memory.
    c. how rapidly participants can "look up" a word in their "mental dictionary."
    d. the content of a participant's memory nodes.

Answer: c

14. In trial 18 of a lexical-decision task, a participant sees the word "chair." Of the following, which will produce the strongest priming for this trial?
    a. In trial 17, the stimulus presented was "care."
    b. In trial 17, the stimulus presented was "table."

c. In trial 17, the stimulus presented was "fair."

d. In trial 17, the stimulus presented was "tree."

Answer: b

15. Participants are asked their mother's first name and then their father's first name. Their answers to the second question will be:

a. faster because activation spreads between two well-connected nodes.

b. faster because the first answer will be locally represented.

c. slower because of semantic interference.

d. slower because of fan effects.

Answer: a

16. The priming effect observed in lexical-decision procedures reflects all of the following *except*:

a. nodes are activated individually, so the activation of each node is largely independent of the activation level of neighboring nodes.

b. once a node is activated, activation is likely to spread to other nodes, representing semantically related concepts.

c. a node can be more quickly activated if it has already received some subthreshold activation from neighboring nodes.

d. activation is likely to spread between closely associated nodes and is unlikely to spread between more distantly related nodes.

Answer: a

17. In a sentence-verification task, participants respond to these two sentences: "A canary has feathers," and "A canary is yellow." We should predict faster response times to the second sentence because:

a. participants are slowed by semantic ambiguity.

b. participants' responses are faster to perceptual properties than to conceptual ones.

c. participants are faster in judging "isa" associations than they are in judging "hasa" associations.

d. the property of having feathers is associated with the bird node, not the canary node.

Answer: d

18. Sentence-verification tasks are typically used:

a. to assess the extent of participants' knowledge about a topic.

b. to probe for a participant's false beliefs.

c. to determine how swiftly participants can access routine, everyday knowledge.

d. to quantify the contribution of schemata to memory errors.

Answer: c

19. In a sentence-verification task, a participant sees sentences such as "A penguin is a bird," or "A dog is an animal." Generally, these sentences are of the form "An X is a Y." The speed of a participant's response to these sentences will be slower if:
    a. several associative links must be traversed to trace a path between the node for X and the node for Y.
    b. the participants have recently seen the items named (e.g., penguin or dog).
    c. the object named by X is a typical member of the category named by Y.
    d. there is a direct connection between the nodes for X and the nodes for Y.

    Answer: a

20. The concept of "degree of fan" refers to:
    a. the relationship between thoughts and concepts.
    b. the speed with which a node will respond to a given input.
    c. how many associative links radiate out from a node.
    d. the rate at which activation of a node returns to baseline levels.

    Answer: c

21. Node L within a memory network has a low degree of fan. Node H within the network has a high degree of fan. All other things equal, a comparison of the nodes will show that Node H:
    a. will, when activated, send activation to a smaller number of neighbors.
    b. will, when activated, send less activation to each of its associated nodes.
    c. can be reached via a smaller number of retrieval paths.
    d. has a higher response threshold.

    Answer: b

22. Marni knows many facts about cowboy hats. However, while each of these facts is associated with "cowboy hats," the various facts are *not* associated with one another. As a result, Marni may be *less able* to recall a particular fact about cowboy hats in comparison to someone who knows just that fact and nothing more. This is because:
    a. activation spreads to only one node at a time, so the process of spread will take too long, and Marni will give up before she finds the sought after information.
    b. there are simply too many nodes to access.
    c. all of Marni's facts will become activated at once, causing anterograde amnesia.
    d. the large degree of fan from her cowboy hat node causes the activation to be spread too thinly over the numerous connected nodes for it to activate the node she needs.

    Answer: d

23. A search through memory can be launched in several different ways. Which of the following is *not* one of these ways?
    a. A stimulus is detected by the appropriate input nodes, and the nodes then trigger other nodes within the memory network.
    b. A participant is contemplating an idea, and the nodes representing the idea then send activation to related nodes.
    c. A participant is remembering an event she once witnessed, and activation then spreads outward from the memory nodes representing the event.
    d. The memory executive identifies the focus of the memory question and directs activation toward the address of the target material.

    Answer: d

24. In a "winner-takes-all" system:
    a. a stronger node inhibits a weaker node, so that the stronger node gets even more activation than its (already larger) share.
    b. a weaker node can beat out a stronger node by inhibiting the stronger node.
    c. all activation flows toward a stronger node.
    d. only the strongest node inhibits other nodes.

    Answer: a

25. Which of the following is an advantage of a "winner-takes-all" system?
    a. it allows the largest possible number of nodes to be activated.
    b. it prevents stronger nodes from excessively inhibiting the input of weaker nodes.
    c. it provides a selective mechanism that reduces "noise" in one's thoughts.
    d. it promotes activation of side-thoughts, which in turn promotes the discovery of novel associations.

    Answer: c

26. Which of the following is a *dis*advantage of a "winner-takes-all" system?
    a. It doesn't allow a person to concentrate her thoughts on one topic.
    b. If a person's thoughts get sidetracked, she may have trouble getting back to the main point.
    c. It tends to prevent thoughts from being followed through to their completion.
    d. It wastes energy on excessive activation and inhibition.

    Answer: b

27. In associative-network modeling, beliefs and memories are contained within:
    a. the individual nodes.
    b. template-like structures.
    c. the pattern of connections, independent of current activation states.
    d. the current state of activation of the relevant nodes.

    Answer: c

28. Which of the following is not a proposition?
    a. My son eats too much candy.
    b. All children eat too much candy.
    c. All children despise candy.
    d. too much candy

    Answer: d

29. In Anderson's network account of propositional knowledge:
    a. propositions are encoded by means of a small number of types of links, such as "isa" links or "hasa" links.
    b. propositions are linked to an image depicting the proposition's contents.
    c. associations are identified in terms of their syntactic role within the proposition.
    d. propositions are limited to simple sentences such as "Dogs eat bones," or "My son fed the pigeons."

    Answer: c

30. Which of the following is most important in allowing network models to represent episodic knowledge, in contrast to more general knowledge?
    a. type nodes, specifying the context in which an event took place
    b. agent nodes, identifying the main participants in an event
    c. input nodes, tying propositions to perceptual qualities
    d. token nodes, representing specific instances of a category

    Answer: d

31. The term "homunculus" refers to:
    a. the intelligent "little person in the head" who directs our mental functioning.
    b. the inhibitory mechanism that prevents overly broad activation of the memory network
    c. the device needed to launch searches through the memory network.
    d. an element of computer modeling of knowledge needed to direct the processing of new knowledge.

    Answer: a

32. Psychologists seek to avoid claims about the homunculus because:
    a. we are still uncertain which parts of the brain support the homunculus's function.
    b. the claims serve merely as IOUs, since the functioning of the homunculus itself still needs to be explained.
    c. it is extremely difficult to test specific claims made about the homunculus.
    d. evidence suggests that not all individuals have a homunculus.

    Answer: b

33 .One might be tempted to include a homunculus within one's theorizing because:
   a. neuroimaging studies indicate homunculus-like structures.
   b. memory search sometimes seems less mechanical than a network theory seems to imply.
   c. sophisticated mechanisms seem needed in order to establish the initial connections among nodes.
   d. computer models including a homunculus have been more successful in simulating human memory than have models without a homunculus.

Answer: b

34. The term "connectionism" refers to:
   a. the study of communicative connections among individual neurons.
   b. a programming technique useful in simulating human memory.
   c. the phenomena observed when cognitive schemata interact with visual inputs.
   d. the claim that complex cognitive phenomena are best understood in terms of the parallel operation of many local and unsophisticated processes.

Answer: d

35. Connectionist (or PDP) models differ from classic associative networks in that connectionism:
   a. employs distributed processes.
   b. relies on a central executive to coordinate processing.
   c. uses local representations rather than distributed representations.
   d. draws mostly on serial processing.

Answer: a

36. In a system using "distributed representations," each idea or mental content:
   a. is represented by a single node.
   b. is represented by a group of nodes, so that the nodes are active only when the particular content is being contemplated.
   c. is represented by means of a widespread pattern of activation involving many different nodes.
   d. is represented by many different nodes, so that the content is brought to mind whenever any of the nodes is activated.

Answer: c

37. In order for a connectionist (or PDP) network to function, each of the nodes must function:
   a. in parallel with all of the other nodes.
   b. in a fashion coordinated by the central executive.
   c. in a manner that makes sophisticated use of the information available to that node.

    d. only when the specific content assigned to that node is relevant to the ongoing operation.

Answer: a

38. In connectionist theorizing, the strength of the association between two nodes is referred to as the association's:
    a. activation strength.
    b. associativity.
    c. activation potential.
    d. connection weight.

Answer: d

39. At this moment, Enriqueta is thinking about her garden. In network terms, this "thinking about garden" is directly reflected in:
    a. the connection weights among the nodes representing "garden."
    b. the activation levels of the nodes representing "garden."
    c. the response thresholds for the nodes representing "garden."
    d. a temporary change in the connection weights among the nodes representing "garden."

Answer: b

40. In a connectionist model, "knowledge" is best defined as:
    a. a state of activation.
    b. a potential for activation, when present, to flow in a certain way.
    c. a particular group of nodes.
    d. the potential for creating new connections among nodes.

Answer: b

41. Martha knows that London is the capital of England, but at this moment she is thinking about neither London nor England. In network terms, this bit of knowledge about London is best reflected in:
    a. the current activation levels within the nodes representing London.
    b. the response thresholds for the nodes for London and England.
    c. the pattern of how activation will flow once the nodes representing London are activated.
    d. the degree of fan for the nodes for England.

Answer: c

42. Connectionist theorists have proposed that connection weights are determined:
    a. genetically.
    b. by learning algorithms driven entirely by local forces.
    c. by a central processor.
    d. randomly.

Answer: b

43. The strength of connections are often adjusted with reference to an "error signal." This signal:
    a. is computed by comparing the output produced to the output desired.
    b. is provided by social interaction with other network theorists.
    c. is used in an inverse fashion, such that connection strengths are adjusted least when the signal is at its maximum.
    d. causes the network to slow down whenever an error is made.

    Answer: a

44. Researchers are divided in their assessments of connectionist models. Which of the following is *not* a concern that has been raised about these models?
    a. There has been some debate about the biological realism of the models.
    b. Some have argued that connectionist models can accomplish complex tasks only when the input, or teaching examples, is adjusted in precisely the right way.
    c. So far, connectionist models have been able to accomplish only narrowly defined tasks and have not achieved the broad intelligence displayed by humans.
    d. Connectionist models seem limited in the quantity of information they can store and function best when the knowledge relevant to a task is limited in scope.

    Answer: d

CHAPTER 9 | Concepts and Generic Knowledge

1. It seems unlikely that our conceptual knowledge is represented by "mental definitions" because:
   a. each person has his or her own idea about how concepts should be defined.
   b. many of our abstract concepts ("justice," "love," "God") are difficult to define.
   c. it is easy to find exceptions to any definition proposed.
   d. most of our concepts are difficult to express in words.

   Answer: c

2. Categorization models based on family resemblance rely on:
   a. the definition of each category.
   b. feature overlap among the members of a category.
   c. the necessary conditions for membership in a category.
   d. the sufficient conditions for membership in a category.

   Answer: b

3. When we say, "There is a family resemblance among all the members of the Martinez family," this means that:
   a. there is at least one feature shared by all the members of the family.
   b. there is at least one identifying trait such that if you have that trait, you are certain to be a member of the family.
   c. any pair of family members will have certain traits in common even though there may be no traits shared by all of the family members.
   d. there are several features that all members of the family have in common.

   Answer: c

4. According to prototype theory, the mental representation for each concept:
   a. represents an average or ideal for the category's members.
   b. specifies the necessary and sufficient conditions for category membership.
   c. is a definition of the category's center.
   d. lists the perceptual features that are found only in that category.

   Answer: a

5. The claim that mental categories have "fuzzy boundaries" is a claim that:
   a. researchers have been unable to specify the boundaries for the categories people use every day.
   b. different individuals have somewhat different concepts, making it easy for people to disagree about how a particular object should be categorized.
   c. the boundaries for a general category are less clear-cut than are the boundaries for a basic-level category.
   d. category membership is a matter of degree, not an all-or-nothing distinction.

   Answer: d

6. The claim that mental categories have "graded membership" is a claim that:
   a. one can not specify precisely whether or not a test case is in the category.
   b. some category members are better suited than others as category members.
   c. a participant's belief about a category's membership shifts as the participant learns more about the category.
   d. many category members approach the ideal for that category.

   Answer: b

7. In trial 18 of a sentence-verification task participants see the sentence "A robin is a bird." In trial 42 they see "A penguin is a bird." According to prototype theory, we should expect:
   a. faster responses to "robin" because participants more readily see the resemblance between "robin" and the bird prototype.
   b. faster responses to "robin" because of response priming
   c. faster responses to "penguin" because penguins are higher in typicality.
   d. faster responses to "penguin" because participants are helped by the contrast between "penguin" and the bird prototype.

   Answer: a

8. If asked to name as many birds as they can, participants are most likely to name:
   a. larger birds (e.g., hawk, owl).
   b. distinctive birds (e.g., vulture, penguin).
   c. birds associated with other familiar concepts (e.g., turkey, bald eagle).
   d. birds resembling the prototype (e.g., robin, sparrow).

   Answer: d

9. There is a pattern of "converging evidence" in the evidence showing graded category membership. This means that:
   a. different individuals agree in their identification of typical category members.
   b. the same category members turn out to be privileged in a wide range of experimental tasks.
   c. more recent studies have allowed a more precise specification of which category members are typical.
   d. as children grow up they gain a more specific notion of what it is that identifies each category.

   Answer: b

10. Participants are asked which birds they think are "particularly birdy" and which birds are "not very birdy." We should expect that the birds judged as "birdiest" are:
    a. birds rarely mentioned in a production task.
    b. birds that are infrequent in the participants' environment.
    c. birds identified quickly in a picture-identification task.
    d. birds not likely to be identified as typical.

    Answer: c

11. The term "basic-level category" refers to:
    a. the level of categorization regarded by most participants as indisputable.
    b. the most general level of categorization participants can think of.
    c. the most specific level of categorization participants can think of.
    d. the most natural level of categorization, neither too specific nor too general.

    Answer: d

12. Basic-level categories have all of the following traits *except*:
    a. if asked simply to describe an object, participants are likely to use the basic-level term.
    b. basic-level categories are usually represented in the language via a single word.
    c. basic-level descriptions are more difficult to remember than are more general descriptions.
    d. basic-level terms are acquired by children at a younger age than are either more specific or more general terms.

    Answer: c

13. According to "exemplar-based theories" of mental categories, participants identify an object by comparing it to:
    a. a prototype.
    b. a single remembered instance of the category.

c. a definition.

d. a mental image.

Answer: b

14. An important difference between "categorization via exemplars" and "categorization via prototypes" is that according to exemplar theory:
    a. the standard used in categorization can vary from one situation to the next.
    b. one categorizes objects by comparing them to a mentally represented standard.
    c. categorization depends on a judgment of resemblance.
    d. categories are represented in the mind by a relatively concrete illustration of the category.

Answer: a

15. When categorization judgments draw on remembered exemplars, the participant is probably being influenced by the type of memory we call:
    a. memory schemata.
    b. implicit memory.
    c. generic memory.
    d. sensory memory.

Answer: b

16. According to exemplar theory, typicality effects:
    a. are difficult to explain.
    b. reflect the fact that typical category members are probably frequent in our environment and are therefore frequently represented in memory.
    c. are produced by the fact that the exemplars in memory for each category tend to resemble each other.
    d. should be observed with categories having homogeneous membership, but not with more variable categories.

Answer: b

17. In making category judgments, we are often sensitive to the degree of variability within the target category. This fact is easily explained:
    a. by exemplar-based theories, but not by prototype theory.
    b. by prototype theory, but not by exemplar-based theories.
    c. by neither prototype theory nor exemplar-based theories.
    d. by both prototype theory and exemplar-based theories.

Answer: a

18. In many procedures, participants are sensitive to a category's degree of variability. It seems likely that this is so because they refer to:
    a. some mental representation of the average for that category.
    b. some mental representation of a direct estimate of variability.

    c. a small number of examples of the category's members, allowing them to estimate the range of "what's possible" within the category.

    d. the full set of the category's members, allowing them to assess directly the range of possibilities within the category.

Answer: c

19. Most birds have short legs, and most birds have short bills. However, if a bird has long legs, it is also likely to have a long bill. This last fact is easily represented in:

    a. both a prototype and an exemplar-based representation.

    b. neither a prototype nor an exemplar-based representation.

    c. a prototype, but not in an exemplar-based representation.

    d. in an exemplar-based representation, but not in a prototype.

Answer: d

20. Judgments about which category members are typical and which are not:

    a. are easily shifted by changes in context or changes in perspective.

    b. shift as one learns more about the category but then become quite stable.

    c. differ sharply from one individual to the next.

    d. are impressively constant across individuals and situations.

Answer: a

21. A researcher makes up a new category: "Personal items that you probably wouldn't take with you on a vacation." Categories such as these:

    a. rarely show the graded-membership pattern.

    b. are likely to have clearer category boundaries than do more familiar categories.

    c. are likely to show a graded-membership pattern.

    d. are difficult for participants to use in judgment tasks.

Answer: c

22. To explain the graded-membership pattern in ad hoc categories, it seems best to argue that:

    a. participants are able to generate new category prototypes whenever they need them.

    b. participants are able to generate definitions for the artificial categories.

    c. participants judge these categories by considering the history of the category members.

    d. participants can think of no exemplars for the artificial categories and therefore must rely on prototypes.

Answer: a

23. Reuben is visiting the aquarium and has just seen an octopus for the very first time. Reuben is therefore likely to have:

a. a definition for the concept "octopus."
b. only exemplar-based knowledge for the concept "octopus."
c. a prototype for the "octopus" concept.
d. a prototype for the "octopus" concept and some exemplar-based knowledge.

Answer: b

24. Researchers have claimed that as one gains more and more experience with a category, the mental representation for that category is likely to shift:
a. from a prototype to exemplar-based knowledge.
b. from exemplar-based knowledge to a definition.
c. from a definition to a prototype.
d. from exemplar-based knowledge to a prototype.

Answer: d

25. A student is just beginning to learn about the diagnostic category "schizophrenia." For this student, it will be easiest to recognize a schizophrenic if the test case:
a. matches the prototype for a schizophrenic individual.
b. resembles the average of the specific cases the student has already encountered.
c. resembles one of the specific cases the student has already encountered.
d. resembles none of the specific cases the student has already encountered.

Answer: c

26. Research with highly experienced dermatologists indicates that these experts:
a. are influenced by recently viewed exemplars.
b. rely almost exclusively on the definition of a diagnostic category.
c. are no longer influenced by exemplar-based knowledge.
d. do not employ prototypes in their diagnoses.

Answer: a

27. In making judgments about category membership, participants:
a. base their judgments entirely on a stimulus's typicality.
b. will not judge a stimulus to be in the category unless the stimulus resembles the category prototype or category exemplars.
c. are often able to make a distinction between typicality and actual category membership.
d. generally base their judgment on factors other than typicality.

Answer: c

28. In one procedure, participants were asked to judge which was a "better" even number, four or eighteen. The participants:
a. were unable to perform this absurd task.

b. offered judgments that show that well-defined categories do not show the graded-membership pattern.

c. regarded all of the even numbers as being "equivalently even."

d. made the judgment in a fashion that implied a graded-membership pattern for the category "even number."

Answer: d

29. Participants know that penguins are not typical birds, but they are certain that penguins are birds. This indicates that judgments about category membership:

a. depend on a judgment of typicality.

b. are not settled entirely by an assessment of typicality.

c. are independent of typicality.

d. do not conform to the requirements of a definition.

Answer: b

30. The textbook's discussion of "mutilated lemons" and "perfect counterfeits" implies all of the following *except* that:

a. an object can be in a category even if the object has no resemblance to the category's prototype.

b. an object can be excluded from a category even if the object has a strong resemblance to the category's prototype.

c. the history of an object is sometimes crucial in determining the object's category membership.

d. participants are unable to separate their judgments about category membership from their judgments about typicality.

Answer: d

31. Evidence suggests that preschool children seem to believe that:

a. no matter how you changed a skunk's behavior or appearance, it would still be a skunk and not a raccoon.

b. it is behavior that matters for category identity, so if a skunk learned to act like a raccoon, it would count as a genuine raccoon.

c. it is appearance that matters for category identity, so if a skunk were altered to look like a raccoon, it would count as a genuine raccoon.

d. it is the combination of behavior and appearance that matters for category identity, so both attributes would have to be changed to turn one organism into another.

Answer: a

32. Categorization is plainly influenced by judgments about resemblance, but it is also influenced by factors *other than* resemblance. Which of the following is *not* part of the evidence indicating the importance of these other factors?

a. People sometimes judge an object to be in a category despite the fact that the object has virtually zero resemblance to other objects in that category.

b. Resemblance plays a key role in the use of prototypes, but plays no role in the well-documented use of exemplars.

c. Resemblance is typically determined by relatively superficial perceptual features, but sometimes categorization depends on "deeper" essential features of the category.

d. In order to make judgments according to resemblance, we must be guided by other beliefs; otherwise, our judgments of resemblance might be guided by irrelevant attributes of the object.

Answer: b

33. The text points out that plums and lawn mowers share many traits. This suggests that:
a. there is a strong resemblance between plums and lawn mowers.
b. resemblance is not influenced by shared traits.
c. in judging resemblance, we must determine which traits matter and which do not.
d. distinctive traits, not shared traits, determine resemblance judgments.

Answer: c

34. An "identification heuristic" is a strategy:
a. that allows swift categorization of a target even if the strategy risks occasional error.
b. that seeks accurate categorization even if the strategy is sometimes inefficient.
c. that relies on a web of background knowledge in categorizing objects.
d. that uses prototypes to promote accurate identifications.

Answer: a

35. In general, a "heuristic" is a strategy that:
a. we use when we are particularly concerned about accuracy.
b. allows efficiency even if this implies a risk of occasional error.
c. uses background knowledge to allow swifter processing.
d. has been well practiced so that it can be used automatically.

Answer: b

36. Judgments according to typicality work well as an identification heuristic. Which of the following does *not* contribute to the success of this heuristic?
a. Typicality is often determined by relatively superficial features, and these features can be judged quickly.
b. Judgments based on typicality can lead to error, since typicality is not the same as category membership.

    c. Objects that resemble a typical category member are likely to be members of that category.

    d. Judgments about typicality usually draw on only part of our conceptual knowledge and thus provide a streamlined basis for making judgments.

Answer: b

37. Several scholars have proposed that concepts must be understood in the context of "mental models" or "implicit theories." This perspective implies all of the following *except* that:

    a. in order to understand an individual concept, we need to understand the concept in the context of other, related concepts.

    b. our understanding of a concept includes a definition of the concept but is not limited to that definition.

    c. our beliefs about a concept indicate which aspects of the concept are essential and which are not.

    d. the meaning of a concept is determined by a network of other beliefs.

Answer: b

38. People are able to judge that an airplane could not be built out of whipped cream, but could (perhaps) be built out of glass. This fact implies that:

    a. humans have complex implicit theories of airplanes and other concepts.

    b. the category "airplane" is a special type of category because we must have outside information to understand it.

    c. a complex prototype theory is needed to explain knowledge, but reference to exemplars is not necessary.

    d. the category "airplane" can be viewed as completely separate from other categories.

Answer: a

CHAPTER 10 | Language

1. The study of the sounds used in language is usually referred to as:
   a. phonology.
   b. semantics.
   c. morphology.
   d. acoustics.

   Answer: a

2. The smallest units of language that carry meaning are called:
   a. morphemes.
   b. phonemes.
   c. phonetic elements.
   d. words.

   Answer: a

3. The relationships among words, and information about a word's role within a sentence, are often specified by:
   a. phonetic segments.
   b. lexical units.
   c. content morphemes.
   d. function morphemes.

   Answer: d

4. Sounds that are produced with the vocal folds vibrating are called:
   a. fricatives.
   b. nasal.
   c. stops.
   d. voiced.

   Answer: d

5. To produce some sounds, the flow of air out of the lungs is interrupted by the lips; for other sounds, the flow is disrupted by the placement of the tongue and teeth. This feature of sound production is referred to as:
   a. place of articulation.
   b. manner of production.
   c. voicing.
   d. speech locus.

   Answer: a

6. In some speech sounds, the flow of air out of the lungs is entirely disrupted; for other sounds, the flow of air is restricted, but air continues to flow. This feature of sound production is referred to as:
   a. place of articulation.
   b. manner of production.
   c. voicing.
   d. speech locus.

   Answer: b

7. The number of phonemes used by the English language is approximately:
   a. 8.
   b. 40.
   c. 150.
   d. several thousand.

   Answer: b

8. In ordinary speech production, the boundaries between syllables or between words are:
   a. usually marked by momentary pauses.
   b. usually marked by slight loudness changes.
   c. usually marked by slight changes in pitch.
   d. usually not marked, so they must be determined by the perceiver.

   Answer: d

9. The process of "slicing" the stream of speech into successive syllables or words is called:
   a. sound segregation.
   b. speech segmentation.
   c. categorical perception.
   d. articulation.

   Answer: b

10. "Coarticulation" refers to the fact that, in producing speech:
    a. the movement of the tongue and lips must be carefully coordinated with the output of air from the lungs.

b. phonemes overlap, both in their actual production and in their sound pattern.

c. a single position of the tongue is used for several different speech sounds.

d. the tongue must be moved into its appropriate position simultaneously with the positioning of the teeth and lips.

Answer: b

11. The perception of speech is made easier by all of the following *except*:

a. there is impressively little variation from one speaker to the next, at least within a single geographic region.

b. the content of the speech we hear is often predictable based on knowledge external to language.

c. the content of the speech we hear is often predictable because of the rules guiding the structure of language.

d. most of the speech we hear employs a relatively small number of words, used over and over.

Answer: a

12. The term "categorical perception" refers to the fact that:

a. we are better at hearing some categories of sounds than we are at hearing other categories.

b. we are skillful at identifying sounds but are less skillful at hearing the physical characteristics of those sounds.

c. we are better at hearing the difference between sounds from different categories than we are at distinguishing sounds from the same category.

d. we are highly sensitive to variations within a category but are less sensitive to the contrast between categories.

Answer: c

13. The term "voice-onset time" (or VOT) refers to:

a. the age at which infants begin to produce vocal sounds.

b. the time that elapses between successive syllables in ordinary speech.

c. the average length of pause between two people's utterances in a conversation.

d. the amount of time that elapses between the moment air begins to flow at the start of speech sound and the moment at which voicing begins.

Answer: d

14. A researcher creates a series of synthetic speech sounds gradually ranging, in uniform small steps, from a "ta" sound at one extreme to a "da" sound at the other extreme. Participants are asked to identify each of these sounds. The researcher should expect to find that:

a. as the sounds gradually shift from "ta" to "da," participants' pattern of responding gradually shifts from "ta" to "da."

    b. participants identify sounds close to "ta" as "ta" and identify sounds close to "da" as "da," but they are unable to identify the sounds midway between these.

    c. participants are able to identify the sounds at the extremes of the range but are confused by all other sounds.

    d. participants' perceptions of the sounds show an abrupt transition, with all of the sounds closer to "ta" clearly identified as "ta," while all of the sounds closer to "da" are clearly identified as "da."

Answer: d

15. The plural for the word "pill" is pronounced with a /z/ sound (it is pronounced "pillz"), but the plural for "pit" is pronounced with an /s/ sound ("pits"). This contrast is governed by a rule of:
    a. syntax.
    b. semantics.
    c. phonology.
    d. pragmatics.

Answer: c

16. "The bright object shining in the daylight sky" is the _____ for the word "sun."
    a. sense
    b. reference
    c. meaning
    d. prototype

Answer: b

17. A word's reference must be distinct from the word's meaning for all of the following reasons *except*:
    a. the meaning of a word or phrase is often just a matter of convention.
    b. the reference of a word is often a matter of accident or coincidence even though the meaning of the phrase is stable.
    c. two words or phrases often have the same reference even though they have different meaning.
    d. some words (e.g., "unicorn") have no reference but still have a meaning.

Answer: a

18. The claim that language is "generative" is a claim that:
    a. it is always possible to generate new sounds to add to the language.
    b. the units of language can be combined and recombined to create vast numbers of new linguistic entities.
    c. language can be used to generate new knowledge and new discoveries.

    d. scholars have been able to invent an unlimited number of new words, allowing them to express any concept they wish.

Answer: b

19. Rules that describe the "proper" way to speak or the way language is "supposed to be" are called:
    a. rules of discourse.
    b. pragmatic rules.
    c. prescriptive rules.
    d. syntax rules.

Answer: c

20. Which of the following is not true about the pattern of linguistic performance?
    a. Performance often contains errors that the speaker knows how to correct.
    b. Performance provides a direct assessment of the extent of one's linguistic knowledge.
    c. Performance is influenced by slips, lapses of attention, and limits of memory.
    d. Performance often omits language patterns that the speaker is able to use, but chooses not to use.

Answer: b

21. Linguistic competence is often revealed by:
    a. reaction-time studies examining how quickly participants can process a sentence.
    b. examination of the speech produced spontaneously by native speakers of a language.
    c. studying which sentences participants find natural or fluent, and which they find awkward.
    d. requesting metalinguistic judgments from a participant.

Answer: d

22. Metacognitive judgments are defined as judgments:
    a. in which one must comment on a mental activity rather than participate in the activity.
    b. requiring careful scrutiny of the available evidence.
    c. in which one comments on the relation between one's own past behaviors and the behaviors of others in the environment.
    d. made immediately after the evidence has become available.

Answer: a

23. The linguistic rules described in the text:
    a. are deliberately followed by speakers of a language.
    b. seem to be innate.
    c. are unconscious but are reliably followed by speakers of the language.
    d. are generally followed, but exceptions to the rules are not difficult to find.

    Answer: c

24. Linguistic rules seem to be the source of children's "over-regularization errors." This sort of error is visible, for example, whenever a child:
    a. uses a regular sequence of words to express an idea even though a different sequence would be more effective.
    b. sees a squirrel and says, "There's a cat!"
    c. says "I goed" or "He runned."
    d. fails to distinguish between similar speech sounds.

    Answer: c

25. The text argues that child's "over-regularization errors" are caused by:
    a. an immature brain.
    b. an over-reliance on a linguistic rule that precedes a mature understanding of when rules apply.
    c. a loss of previous understanding of irregular forms of words.
    d. a lack of (even unconscious) understanding of linguistic rules.

    Answer: b

26. The rules governing the sequence of words in forming phrases and sentences are rules of:
    a. syntax.
    b. semantics.
    c. phonology.
    d. pragmatics.

    Answer: a

27. Sentences like "Colorless green ideas sleep furiously" indicate that:
    a. not all sentences need to have a verb phrase.
    b. it is possible for a sentence to have an irregular phrase structure.
    c. the semantic content of a sentence governs its syntactic form.
    d. a sentence can be grammatical even if it is meaningless.

    Answer: d

28. The phrase-structure rule "S → NP VP" summarizes the fact that:
    a. whenever a sentence is uttered, it must be followed by a noun phrase and a verb phrase.
    b. the subject of a sentence must specify both a noun phrase and a verb phrase.

c. a sentence can consist of either a noun phrase or a verb phrase.

d. a sentence can consist of a noun phrase followed by a verb phrase.

Answer: d

29. A phrase-structure rule is a rule governing:
    a. whether a proposition is expressed as a declarative sentence or as a question.
    b. whether a proposition is true or false.
    c. what the constituents must be for any syntactic element of a sentence.
    d. what contents can be expressed by a sentence.

Answer: c

30. Recursion is:
    a. a grammatical error often made by preschool children.
    b. a property of a rule system allowing a symbol to appear within its own definition.
    c. a feature of language placing limits on the structure of a sentence.
    d. a processing step needed for speech segmentation.

Answer: b

31. Which of the following claims about phrase-structure rules is *false*?
    a. The rules govern the pattern of branching that is possible in a phrase-structure tree.
    b. The rules determine the meaning of each sentence.
    c. Word sequences that break the rules are likely to be judged as "ungrammatical."
    d. The rules identify "natural" groupings of words within a sentence.

Answer: b

32. Which of the following provides an example of phrase-structure ambiguity?
    a. "I saw the bear with my binoculars." (Who had the binoculars?)
    b. "He paid a lot for the ball." (Round toy or formal party?)
    c. "She loves a good whine." (Can be heard as a "good wine.")
    d. "We saw it." (Reference of "it" unspecified.)

Answer: a

33. Phrase-structure rules allow us to generate an abstract representation of a sentence, which is referred to as its:
    a. sentence trace.
    b. surface structure.
    c. proposition.
    d. underlying structure.

Answer: d

34. Movement rules allow the elements of a sentence to change position, and thus change its:
    a. sentence trace.
    b. surface structure.
    c. proposition.
    d. d-structure.

    Answer: b

35. Certain properties of language appear to be shared by every language that has ever been studied. These properties are referred to as:
    a. phrase-structure rules.
    b. deep rules.
    c. language parameters.
    d. linguistic universals.

    Answer: d

36. To "parse" a sentence you need to:
    a. figure out the sentence's meaning.
    b. determine if the sentence is true or false.
    c. determine the syntactic role of each word in the sentence.
    d. determine the implications of the sentence.

    Answer: c

37. A "garden-path sentence" is defined as one:
    a. in which words early in the sentence imply one syntactic organization, but words later in the sentence demand a different organization.
    b. that is difficult for participants to parse.
    c. for which no sensible parsing can be specified.
    d. in which the wording is ambiguous, so two different phrase structures can be associated with the sentence.

    Answer: a

38. In some cases, "garden-path sentences" can be very hard to follow. Usually, though, the _____ of the sentence makes it easy to understand.
    a. syntactic organization
    b. noun phrasing
    c. wording
    d. extralinguistic context

    Answer: d

39. Which of the following is not a principle that guides sentence parsing?
    a. Decisions about the parsing of individual words are not made until the entire sentence has been heard.

b. In general, we assume that the sentences we hear will be in the active, not passive, voice.
c. Parsing makes use of the small function words (like "that" and "which") to identify the sentence's phrase structure.
d. The semantics of the sentence are used as an aid in determining who is the source of the action and who is the recipient.

Answer: a

40. The principal of minimal attachment refers to:
   a. a rule of conversation governing how successive statements within a conversation are related to each other.
   b. a principle of speech perception determining the connection between adjacent phonemes.
   c. a heuristic used to determine the referent of pronouns within a sentence.
   d. a processing strategy in which the listener seeks the simplest possible phrase structure that will accommodate the words heard to that point.

Answer: d

41. The claim that language processing is "modular" in nature is a claim that:
   a. a noun phrase must obey the same rules no matter where it appears within a sentence.
   b. each stage of processing proceeds in a fashion not influenced by the workings of other stages.
   c. a sentence can be judged to be grammatical independent of the context in which the sentence is uttered.
   d. the steps of parsing are guided simultaneously by considerations of syntax, semantics, and pragmatics.

Answer: b

42. In speaking, the pattern of pauses and the rise and fall of pitch are technically referred to as:
   a. prosody.
   b. musicality.
   c. stress patterns.
   d. expressiveness.

Answer: a

43. Knowing about how language is ordinarily used is technically called:
   a. pronominalization.
   b. conversational implications.
   c. pragmatics.
   d. psycholinguistics.

Answer: c

44. Disruption of language skills caused by damage to the brain is referred to as:
    a. aphasia.
    b. agnosia.
    c. amnesia.
    d. ataxia.

    Answer: a

45. The pattern of good language comprehension but disrupted production, including "agrammatic" speech, is typically associated with:
    a. congenital anarthria.
    b. Broca's aphasia.
    c. Wernicke's aphasia.
    d. Jackson syndrome.

    Answer: b

46. A patient suffering from anomia is likely to show disruption in:
    a. the comprehension of syntactically complex speech.
    b. the ability to distinguish similar phonemes.
    c. the production of grammatical utterances.
    d. the ability to name various objects.

    Answer: d

47. In the 1950s, the anthropologist Benjamin Whorf argued that our language determines the possible range of our thoughts. In the subsequent decades, Whorf's theories:
    a. have been repeatedly supported, with examples including evidence that color vocabulary influences color perception.
    b. have been supported by the discovery that there are 300 Aleut words for snow.
    c. have found little specific support, with current theorists preferring instead to claim that language *guides* our thoughts and memories.
    d. seem correct for some domains (e.g., color perception) but not for other domains (e.g., thinking about spatial relations).

    Answer: c

CHAPTER 11 | Visual Knowledge

1. A psychologist asks her experimental participants to describe their experiences in using mental imagery. The psychologist is collecting:
   a. sentence-verification results.
   b. self-report data.
   c. chronometric evidence.
   d. converging evidence.

   Answer: b

2. When participants are asked to report on their imagery experience, we discover that:
   a. imagery is employed less often than researchers have proposed.
   b. many individuals prefer not to use mental imagery.
   c. participants differ widely in how they describe the experience.
   d. visual imagery is a skill shared by all people.

   Answer: c

3. Chronometric studies:
   a. rely on the fact that mental processes, while quick, do take a measurable amount of time.
   b. have been relatively uninformative for the study of complex mental events.
   c. have documented the descriptive (language-like) properties of mental imagery.
   d. require an understanding of the brain events underlying a particular mental function.

   Answer: a

4. Which of the following claims is true for a depiction of a cat, but not a description of a cat?
   a. Properties strongly associated with the cat (such as whiskers) will be particularly prominent.

    b. The position of the cat (e.g., standing or sitting) does not have to be specified.

    c. Aspects of the cat that are obvious (e.g., the fact that the cat has a body) are likely not to be prominent.

    d. The cat's head will probably be prominent, but the cat's claws are likely not to be.

Answer: d

5. One group of participants is instructed to imagine a cat and the participants are then asked several yes/no questions about their image. A second group of participants is instructed simply to think about cats, with no mention of imagery, and the participants are then asked the same yes/no questions. We should expect that participants responding on the basis of the image will respond more quickly to:

    a. "Does the cat have a head?"

    b. "Does the cat have whiskers?"

    c. "Is the cat a mammal?"

    d. "Does the cat have claws?"

Answer: a

6. According to chronometric studies, information that is prominent in a mental image:

    a. tends to concern aspects that are strongly associated with, or distinctive for, the imaged object.

    b. matches the pattern of information prominent in a description of the imaged object.

    c. corresponds well with the information that is prominent in an actual picture.

    d. is similar to the information prominent in other forms of mental representation.

Answer: c

7. Studies of image scanning indicate that:

    a. participants' scanning rate is slow for short distances but is faster for greater distances.

    b. there is a linear function linking scanning distances and scanning times.

    c. fastest scanning times tend to be obtained with moderate scanning distances.

    d. participants are able to scan across their image virtually instantaneously.

Answer: b

8. A researcher asks a participant to memorize a city map. On the map, the library and the school are 2 inches apart; the school and the hospital are 4

inches apart. The researcher now instructs the participant to form an image of the map, and the researcher determines that the participant needs 1.2 seconds to scan from the library to the school. Which of the following is a reasonable estimate of the time needed to scan from the school to the hospital?
a. 1.2 seconds
b. 0.9 seconds
c. 2.8 seconds
d. 2.4 seconds

Answer: d

9. Participants are given a task that requires them to zoom in on a mental image in order to inspect a detail. Evidence indicates that:
a. the greater the distance to be zoomed, the more time required.
b. the shorter the distance to be zoomed, the more time required.
c. zooming in on an image is a virtually instantaneous process.
d. there is no regular relationship between amount of zoom and the time required.

Answer: a

10. Studies of image scanning indicate that:
a. points close together on the imaged object are apparently physically close in the mental image itself.
b. mental images preserve some spatial relations (e.g., proximity) but not others (e.g., alignment or the relationship of one point being between two others).
c. points close together on the imaged object are functionally close in the mental image.
d. mental images are literally pictures in the brain.

Answer: c

11. Studies of mental rotation indicate that:
a. participants are able to imagine rotation of a two-dimensional display but are unable to imagine rotation in depth.
b. the greater the degree of rotation required, the more time needed to complete the rotation.
c. participants seem able to compare objects in mental imagery without bothering to imagine these objects rotated into alignment.
d. imagined rotation in depth is appreciably faster than imagined rotation in two dimensions.

Answer: b

12. Segal and Fusella asked their participants to visualize one stimulus while attempting to detect a different, rather faint, signal. The data indicate that the activity of visualization:
    a. disrupted the detection of a visual signal but had little impact on the detection of an auditory signal.
    b. served to prime the visual system, promoting detection of the signal.
    c. served as a general distractor, thereby disrupting detection of either a visual or an auditory signal.
    d. had no impact on the detection of the signal.

    Answer: a

13. In some studies, participants have been asked to visualize a particular stimulus in a particular location. If a stimulus is then presented in exactly that location, visualization:
    a. has no effect, even though visualization disrupts detection of stimuli in other positions.
    b. primes perception, independent of the stimulus's identity.
    c. disrupts perception of the stimulus.
    d. serves to prime perception of the stimulus if the stimulus is the one participants were visualizing.

    Answer: d

14. Studies of moment-by-moment brain activity indicate that:
    a. the activity of visualization produces widespread activation of the brain, particularly in the left hemisphere.
    b. the brain regions needed for visualization are distinct from the brain regions needed for actual vision.
    c. when participants are visualizing, activity levels are high in brain regions also crucial for visual perception.
    d. different people employ different brain areas to support their visualizing.

    Answer: c

15. Damage to brain areas needed for vision:
    a. usually has little impact on visualizing.
    b. generally has opposite effects on visualizing and on vision.
    c. is likely to destroy altogether the patient's ability to visualize.
    d. often has disruptive effects for visualizing similar to the disruption observed for visual perception.

    Answer: d

16. The technique of "transcranial magnetic stimulation" employs strong magnetic pulses at a particular site on the scalp. When it is used on the scalp near area V1, the effect is:
    a. to give the participant mild hallucinations.

b. a temporary disruption of vision, but *not* visual imagery.

c. a permanent disruption of visual imagery, and therefore use of the technique is unethical.

d. a temporary disruption of vision *and* visual imagery.

Answer: d

17. Visual acuity is defined as the ability:
    a. to visualize objects with picture-like clarity.
    b. to discern fine detail.
    c. to detect very dim lights.
    d. to differentiate between two similar colors.

Answer: b

18. Evidence indicates that the acuity in visual imagery is:
    a. better than acuity in actual vision.
    b. uniform across the entire image.
    c. similar to acuity in actual vision, with better acuity at the center than at the periphery.
    d. similar to acuity in actual vision, with better acuity at the top than at the bottom.

Answer: c

19. Studies of participants blind since birth indicate that:
    a. their imagery abilities, like their other senses, are superior to those of sighted individuals.
    b. their performance on imagery tasks is similar to the performance of sighted individuals.
    c. blind participants are unable to perform most tasks requiring mental imagery.
    d. participants can do most so-called imagery tasks without using imagery at all.

Answer: b

20. Participants are asked to perform an imagery task while simultaneously keeping track of a visual target (a light that varies in brightness). The visual task:
    a. will disrupt the imagery task.
    b. will have no effect on the imagery task.
    c. will disrupt the imagery task if it requires visual imagery, but not if the task can be done with spatial imagery.
    d. will cause the images to be less vivid but will have no other effects.

Answer: c

21. B. J. is a brain-damaged individual who has lost the ability to do most visual tasks, including tasks requiring him to think about an object's color. Based on other evidence, it is likely that:
    a. B. J. may still be able to perform normally on spatial tasks.
    b. B. J. will also be unable to do auditory tasks, including tasks requiring him to think about pitch.
    c. B. J. will also be unable to do image scanning or mental rotation tasks.
    d. B. J. will also be unable to use imagery mnemonics.

    Answer: a

22. Studies of individual differences in mental-imagery ability indicate that:
    a. women tend to be poor in visual skills, relative to men.
    b. individuals seem not to differ with regard to their imagery skills.
    c. "good" imagers do well on all imagery tasks, while "less good" imagers have a consistent disadvantage in imagery tasks.
    d. each individual has his or her own profile of imagery skills that he or she can do well and that he or she does poorly.

    Answer: d

23. Participants' self-reports about their "imagery vividness":
    a. are correlated with their performance on visual tasks but not with their performance on spatial tasks.
    b. are generally uncorrelated with performance on imagery tasks.
    c. seem to represent only the manner in which participants describe their imagery and do not represent actual differences in the imagery experience.
    d. are correlated with the ease with which participants can do mental rotation tasks.

    Answer: a

24. In some studies, self-reported "vivid imagers" and self-reported "non-imagers" have both been asked to form certain mental images. During this activity, researchers monitored blood flow in the brain. The data show that, during imagery:
    a. both groups show similar levels of blood flow to areas of the brain associated with vision.
    b. the "vivid imagers" show greater blood flow to areas of the brain associated with vision.
    c. the "vivid imagers" showed reduced blood flow to areas of the brain associated with vision.
    d. the "vivid imagers" show greater blood flow to all areas of the brain.

    Answer: b

25. The text considers various arguments concerning the nature of pictures and the nature of percepts. According to the text:
    a. percepts are descriptions, pictures are depictions.
    b. percepts are depictions, pictures are descriptions.
    c. pictures are ambiguous, percepts are organized and thus unambiguous.
    d. pictures are organized and thus unambiguous, percepts are ambiguous.

    Answer: c

26. Evidence indicates that:
    a. discoveries flow easily from mental imagery provided that the discoveries are compatible with the image's reference frame.
    b. mental imagery rarely serves as a source for creative discovery.
    c. participants have enormous difficulty in finding new forms in their own mental images.
    d. participants have an easier time making discoveries from their own mental images if the discoveries require a shift in the image's reference frame.

    Answer: a

27. One group of participants is asked to form an image of "four columns of dots, with each column containing three dots." A second group is asked to form an image of "four rows of dots, with each row containing four dots." We should expect that participants in the second group ("four rows") will:
    a. not differ from participants in the first group because even though the descriptions differ, the depicted images do not.
    b. form a clearer image because their image contains more units.
    c. have an easier time reinterpreting their image.
    d. take longer to form the image because the image contains a large number of units (four rows rather than three columns).

    Answer: d

28. Researchers have argued that visual images are created by:
    a. activating large-scale "templates" in long-term memory.
    b. following "recipes" for the image construction, with the recipes drawn from "image files" in long-term memory.
    c. activating the relevant neurons on the retina.
    d. activating nodes within long-term memory that happen to be associated with sensory information.

    Answer: b

29. The text argues that "image files" in long-term memory:
    a. are distinctive because special processes (like scanning or zooming) operate on them.
    b. hold large-scale "templates" indicating how the imaged form looks.

    c. are encoded, represented, and accessed in the same fashion as any other memory.

    d. usually contain less information than is represented in the active image.

Answer: c

30. An "image file" refers to:

    a. the information that can be derived from a close inspection of a mental image.

    b. the portion of long-term storage that contains all of one's knowledge about visual appearances.

    c. the memory representation of a basic element of visual appearance, such as the representation for "red" or "circular."

    d. descriptive information in long-term memory used as the basis for creating an active image.

Answer: d

31. In one study, participants were asked about the relative spatial positions of Seattle and Montreal. Results suggested that:

    a. this type of simple geography question cannot tell us anything useful about visual imagery or visual memory.

    b. some spatial information is stored in memory in a propositional form rather than an image form.

    c. people are great at reading visual images, and can discover surprising facts in them.

    d. people are miserably bad at reading visual images, and so images are no help in this type of problem.

Answer: b

32. Vera has a large color vocabulary and knows, for example, words that allow her to name a dozen different shades of green. Laura has a much narrower color vocabulary and knows only the basic color terms (red, green, yellow, etc.). If we test Vera and Laura's ability to remember specific colors, we are likely to find that:

    a. Vera will be more successful in a color-memory task.

    b. Laura will be more successful in a color-memory task.

    c. these two individuals will not differ in their color memory.

    d. Vera will have a better memory, but this reflects her advantage in perceiving colors, and not a genuine memory advantage.

Answer: a

33. In a memory experiment, participants were shown a form that could be interpreted in more than one way. Half the participants were told, "Here is a picture of the sun." Other participants were told, "Here is a picture of a

ship's steering wheel." Some time later, participants were asked to draw the exact form they had seen earlier. The data indicate that:
a. participants' visual memories were distinct from their verbal memories, so participants were uninfluenced by the labels.
b. participants' drawings were biased in a fashion that reflected the labels that the participants had been given earlier.
c. the labels had called attention to the ambiguity of the figures, leading to improved memory accuracy.
d. participants were able to remember only the labels, not the drawings.

Answer: b

34. Research by Paivio has documented that words that evoke images:
a. are easier to memorize.
b. are more difficult to memorize.
c. are more easily confused with one another.
d. are easier to identify.

Answer: a

35. Participants who have been blind since birth:
a. rely on a language-based memory system, not on imagery.
b. are able to use imagery mnemonics and show a memory advantage with easily imaged words.
c. show no memory advantage if asked to memorize easily imaged words.
d. are unable to make use of imagery mnemonics.

Answer: b

36. In using imagery mnemonics, participants often try to form bizarre images. Evidence indicates that the bizarreness in the images:
a. actually has no effect on participants' memories.
b. improves participants' memories only if the bizarre images are mixed together with more common images.
c. consistently helps participants to remember the target material.
d. interferes with participants' ability to remember the target material.

Answer: b

37. In memorizing new material, it is consistently helpful if one imagines the items:
a. interacting with each other in some way.
b. in a bizarre relationship.
c. close to each other, but separated so that each is easily visible.
d. one by one so that the items do not blur together.

Answer: a

38. In memorizing new material, the pattern of "dual coding" refers to:
    a. the strategy of encoding the material from two separate perspectives.
    b. the process of encoding the material on two separate occasions.
    c. steps that lead to both a verbal memory and a visual memory.
    d. the formation of a mental image in which the target item is in two separate relationships with its surrounding context.

    Answer: c

39. Paivio and others have proposed that some types of knowledge are encoded in image-based representations and that other types of knowledge are stored in a verbal form. In addition, it is claimed that:
    a. both forms of representation are more efficiently accessed with words as the memory cues.
    b. the knowledge expressed in image-based representations can not be expressed in verbal form.
    c. information about semantic associations is more easily represented in the image-based format.
    d. image-based knowledge is more efficiently accessed with a picture as the memory cue.

    Answer: d

40. Memory for pictures:
    a. tends to be poor, and participants have difficulty remembering series of pictures that contain more than a dozen presentations.
    b. shows an influence of schematic knowledge, just like memories of other sorts.
    c. is not influenced by rehearsal.
    d. is accurate even for elements of the picture that were not closely attended during the initial encoding.

    Answer: b

41. When participants remember a previously viewed picture, they generally:
    a. remember it as less of a close-up than it actually was.
    b. include objects that were not part of the original scene.
    c. demonstrate boundary extension, remembering the picture as smaller than it actually was.
    d. remember it with great accuracy.

    Answer: a

42. Which of the following claims about face memory is *not* true?
    a. Memory for faces is improved by deep processing.
    b. Memory for faces is improved by rehearsal.
    c. In recognizing a face, the correlation between confidence and memory accuracy is quite strong
    d. In recognizing a face, one can be correct that the stimulus is familiar but wrong about why the stimulus is familiar.

    Answer: c

43. Auditory imagery and auditory memory have much in common with visual imagery and visual memory. But there are also important *differences*, including the fact that:
    a. visual imagery uses many of the same mechanisms as vision, but auditory imagery shares little with hearing.
    b. auditory images are more open to reinterpretation than are visual images.
    c. auditory imagery, but not visual imagery, can employ the "inner ear" and "inner voice."
    d. *ear*witnesses tend to be more accurate than *eye*witnesses.

    Answer: c

CHAPTER 12	Judgment: Drawing Conclusions from Evidence

1. An "inductive judgment" is one in which:
   a. one tries to make predictions about upcoming events based on evidence already available.
   b. one tries to make a cause-and-effect judgment about an observed state of affairs.
   c. one begins with a general statement and asks what other specific claims follow from this.
   d. one begins with specific facts or observations and seeks to draw a general conclusion from them.

   Answer: d

2. Solomon remembers how Jacob acted last weekend, and the weekend before that. Based on this, Solomon is trying to figure out whether there is a pattern to Jacob's actions. Solomon is working on a problem of:
   a. deduction.
   b. induction.
   c. confirmation.
   d. derivation.

   Answer: b

3. A "normative account" is one that:
   a. describes how things typically proceed.
   b. describes the data with no evaluation or judgment.
   c. indicates how things are supposed to proceed.
   d. indicates the pattern of the data, averaging across minor case-by-case variations.

   Answer: c

4. Your doctor has just asked you what sorts of things you eat in your normal, daily diet. After you answer the question, the doctor tells you what you should be eating. Your answer to the doctor was a _____ account of your diet; the doctor then provided a(n) _____ account.
   a. descriptive; normative
   b. descriptive; instructive
   c. normative; declarative
   d. inductive; prescriptive

   Answer: a

5. Which of the following is *not* an example of a frequency judgment?
   a. "You've only worn that shirt once since I gave it to you!"
   b. "I am certain that he is bluffing."
   c. "There certainly are a lot of pizzerias in this neighborhood."
   d. "The number of truly caring physicians is getting smaller and smaller."

   Answer: b

6. Heuristics are strategies that:
   a. sometimes risk error in order to gain efficiency.
   b. are underused, despite their advantages.
   c. protect us from overestimating the frequency of real-life events.
   d. ensure step-by-step procedures for finding correct conclusions.

   Answer: a

7. "I can easily think of the names of several dishonest politicians, so I'm certain there are a lot of dishonest politicians!" This is an example of a judgment relying on:
   a. illusory covariation.
   b. representativeness.
   c. anchoring.
   d. the availability heuristic.

   Answer: d

8. The availability heuristic is a strategy in which:
   a. category frequencies tend to be overestimated.
   b. people base their estimates of frequency on how easily they can think of examples of the relevant category.
   c. people judge frequency by referring to their sense of familiarity with the category.
   d. category frequencies are estimated based on schematic knowledge.

   Answer: b

9. Many of us overestimate our own popularity. This could be because we tend to surround ourselves with people who like us, rather than with people who do not, so it is easier for us think of the names of people who like us than it is to think of the names of our enemies. This overestimation of popularity seems to derive, therefore, from using:
   a. anchoring.
   b. base rates.
   c. the atmosphere pattern.
   d. the availability heuristic.

   Answer: d

10. The availability heuristic:
    a. is a time-consuming strategy, so is employed by participants only when a judgment requires special care.
    b. leads to an overestimation of frequency if category members are particularly difficult to remember.
    c. leads us to underestimate frequency because there are usually more category members beyond the ones we recall.
    d. often leads to correct estimates because availability in memory is generally correlated with frequency in the world.

    Answer: d

11. When we encounter a highly unusual event, we are particularly likely to notice and consider the event. As a consequence:
    a. we are likely to think about how distinctive the event really is, leading us to underestimate the likelihood of this type of event.
    b. we are likely to think about the event as being in its own special category, and so the event will have little impact on our estimates of frequency.
    c. the event will be easy to recall, leading us to overestimate the likelihood of this type of event.
    d. the event will be difficult to recall, leading us to underestimate the likelihood of this type of event.

    Answer: c

12. In several studies, participants have been asked to estimate the frequency of occurrence for various causes of death. The evidence suggests that participants' frequency estimates are strongly influenced by:
    a. whether the cause of death was related to natural forces (e.g., lightning, tornado).
    b. how often the cause of death is discussed in the news media.
    c. whether the cause of death is associated with prolonged suffering.
    d. how well the cause of death fits with participants' schematic knowledge.

    Answer: b

13. Once participants have heard an answer to a question, they show a strong tendency to be influenced by that answer and to use it as a reference point in their subsequent reasoning. This tendency is referred to as:
    a. an availability error.
    b. anchoring.
    c. confirmation bias.
    d. perseveration.

    Answer: b

14. The tendency toward anchoring is:
    a. evident whenever an anchor is present.
    b. not detected if participants see clearly that the anchor was randomly chosen.
    c. observed if the anchor is suggested by an authority figure.
    d. strengthened if participants have a good understanding of the topic they are judging.

    Answer: a

15. A student asks herself, "Have I included enough evidence in this paper to make my arguments persuasive?" For judgments of this sort, participants use:
    a. the availability heuristic.
    b. a relatively crude strategy, relying basically on the number of pages in the paper.
    c. strategies that are more sophisticated than the availability heuristic.
    d. the confirmation strategy.

    Answer: b

16. In using the "representativeness heuristic," participants:
    a. extrapolate from a sample of evidence if the category is homogeneous, but not if the category is heterogeneous.
    b. are sensitive to the sample size and draw conclusions more readily from a large sample.
    c. seem to assume that all instances of the category resemble the prototype or average for that category.
    d. are unable to discriminate actual patterns of covariation.

    Answer: c

17. An employer interviews a job candidate for 15 minutes. Based on this, the employer decides that the candidate will perform well in the job, so he hires her. This is a case of:
    a. a sound decision because the employer is making use of available information.
    b. a sound decision because the employer is employing base rates.

  c. a potential error because the employer is assuming that a small sample of information (the interview) is representative of a broader pattern (job performance).

  d. a potential error because the employer is relying on schema-based reasoning rather than on deduction.

Answer: c

18. Which of the following is an example of the "gambler's fallacy"?
  a. "I know the chances of winning the lottery are small, but someone has to win it, and I could be the one!"
  b. "I've gotten a low number the last eight times I've rolled the dice, so a high number is coming up soon!"
  c. "There's an equal chance for any team to win the league's championship."
  d. "The best strategy at the horse races is to bet in the same way as the crowd is betting."

Answer: b

19. Participants are told "Hospital A has an average of 45 births per day; Hospital B has an average of only 15 births per day." The participants are then asked, "Which hospital is more likely to have a day in which at least 60 percent of the babies born are female?" In answering the question, participants:
  a. seem insensitive to the fact that departures from the average case are more likely with a small sample.
  b. seem insensitive to the fact that departures from the average case are more likely with a larger sample.
  c. correctly realize that departures from the average case are not dependent on hospital size.
  d. answer in a fashion governed by the "law of large numbers."

Answer: a

20. Reasoning from "man who" arguments is usually inappropriate because generalizing from a single case is justified:
  a. only for heterogeneous categories.
  b. only when the sample size is adequate.
  c. only when the base rates are unknown.
  d. only when one is sure that the case is truly typical.

Answer: d

21. In one study, participants were shown a film about a family on welfare. Prior to viewing the film, half of the participants were told that the film showed a highly unusual case. The other participants were told that the film showed a quite typical case. After viewing the film, participants were asked their opinions about welfare. Based on other evidence, we would expect to find that:

a. both groups of participants were influenced equally by the film.

b. neither group of participants was influenced by the film.

c. participants who were told that the case was unusual were less influenced by the film.

d. participants who were told that the case was unusual were not influenced by the film.

Answer: a

22. Before reading about a depressed individual, participants are told that the case is not at all typical. This instruction will:

a. prevent participants from using the representativeness heuristic.

b. encourage participants to use the representativeness heuristic.

c. not affect participants' spontaneous use of the representativeness heuristic.

d. influence participants' willingness to draw conclusions from a single case.

Answer: c

23. Fred is convinced that people who wear sandals can not be trusted. People who wear shoes, though, seem fine to Fred. This is a mistaken belief about:

a. anchoring.

b. covariation.

c. availability.

d. representativeness.

Answer: b

24. According to Tversky and Koehler's "support theory," people's judgments are heavily influenced by:

a. whether an argument is phrased positively or negatively.

b. whether an argument is based on an adequate sample of data.

c. whether a claim is vague or whether it is explicit.

d. whether a claim is based on valid premises or invalid premises.

Answer: c

25. The term "covariation" refers to:

a. the relationship between frequency of objects in the world and their availability in memory.

b. the pattern of evidence leading participants to the gambler's fallacy.

c. a cause-and-effect relationship between two variables.

d. the tendency for one observation to be linked to another observation so that, for example, if one is strong, the other is weak.

Answer: d

26. The term "illusory covariation" refers to an error in which:

a. participants perceive an event as occurring far more often than it actually does.

b. participants perceive two variables as being somehow linked to each other when in fact they are not.

c. participants draw a conclusion based on a biased or small sample of evidence.

d. participants refuse to change their minds even though the available evidence clearly challenges their belief.

Answer: b

27. "Illusory covariations" can be documented in:
   a. novices, but only when the cases being judged are of low importance for the participants.
   b. well-trained professionals, but only when the professionals are making judgments outside of their area of expertise.
   c. novices, but not in experts.
   d. individuals who have years of training in the domain being judged.

Answer: d

28. When asked to judge covariation, participants:
   a. seem to lack the knowledge and skills needed for the task.
   b. perform more accurately if they can supplement the data with their prior experience and knowledge.
   c. provide reasonably accurate estimates if they have no prior beliefs about the data.
   d. do best if the relevant data are easily available to them.

Answer: c

29. The text suggests that illusory covariations arise from the fact that participants:
   a. base their covariation estimates only on the data that are easily available to them, and the selection of cases is often biased.
   b. are generally dogmatic and make their judgments with little regard for the data.
   c. do not know how to compute covariation, so they use an estimation strategy that is little better than guessing.
   d. do not know how to make these judgments, so performance improves once the participant gains some expertise.

Answer: a

30. People tend to be more alert and responsive to evidence that supports their preexisting notions and beliefs than to evidence that challenges these. This effect is called:
   a. confirmation bias.
   b. stereotypy.

c. base rate error.

d. the covariation law.

Answer: a

31. If Tabitha believes that detective shows are more dramatic than hospital shows, then "confirmation bias" would lead her to do all of the following *except*:

a. Tabitha will be more likely to notice a detective show that is dramatic.

b. Tabitha will be more likely to overlook a hospital show that is dramatic.

c. Tabitha will easily remember examples of dramatic detective shows.

d. Tabitha will easily remember examples dramatic hospital shows.

Answer: d

32. A base rate is defined as:

a. information that helps us to identify which specific candidates have a target property.

b. information about the broad likelihood of a particular type of event.

c. information indicating the internal variability of a set or category.

d. information that can be used to diagnose an individual category member.

Answer: b

33. Studies indicate that participants:

a. uniformly neglect base-rate information.

b. overutilize base-rate information even if other compelling information is presented.

c. make sensible use of base-rate information if no other information is available.

d. tend to integrate base-rate information with diagnostic information.

Answer: c

34. Participants tend not to use base-rate information if they are also given:

a. diagnostic information.

b. the prior probabilities.

c. statistical information.

d. information about the random device used to select the test case.

Answer: a

35. Participants are told, "Sam was selected from a group of 70 lawyers and 30 engineers. Sam is 42 years old, has three children, and grew up in a large city. What is the likelihood that Sam is a lawyer?" Participants are likely to respond that there is a:

a. 70 percent chance of Sam being a lawyer because the particulars offered provide no information about Sam's career.

b. 70 percent chance of Sam being a lawyer because the irrelevant information causes participants to ignore the base rate.

    c. 50-50 chance of Sam being a lawyer because the particulars offered provide no information about Sam's career.

    d. 50-50 chance of Sam being a lawyer because in this case participants do not know the relevant base rate.

Answer: c

36. Participants are told, "Susan was selected from a group of 30 lawyers and 70 engineers. Susan is skilled in mathematics but is not very good at expressing herself. Her hobbies include woodworking and fixing old cars; she has little interest in politics or current events." Participants are then asked to estimate the likelihood, expressed in a percentage, that Susan is an engineer. Given this information, the correct answer is likely to be:
    a. lower than 30 percent.
    b. higher than 70 percent.
    c. exactly 70 percent.
    d. between 30 percent and 70 percent.

Answer: b

37. Many people get the flu, but the form known as the Blue Flu is relatively rare, affecting less than one-tenth of one percent of the population. Nevertheless, a diagnostic test indicates that Jane has the Blue Flu, and this diagnostic test has, in the past, been accurate 90 percent of the time. Given this information, the likelihood of Jane having the Blue Flu:
    a. can not be calculated from this information.
    b. is approximately 90 percent.
    c. is approximately 10 percent.
    d. is less than 1 percent.

Answer: c

38. Lucia reported to her father that she saw a hummingbird in their back yard. Her father, however, knows that hummingbirds are extremely rare in that part of the country. In this situation:
    a. the diagnostic information confirms the base rate.
    b. the diagnostic information points toward one conclusion, but the base rate points toward a different conclusion.
    c. the base rate is known, but no diagnostic information is available.
    d. there are two pieces of diagnostic information, but no base rate information.

Answer: b

39. The notion of "satisficing" refers to the fact that:
    a. it is often preferable to select a satisfactory answer to a question rather than taking the time to search for the optimal answer.
    b. participants are more likely to seek a carefully chosen judgment if the problem under scrutiny is personally important for the participant.

c. participants' judgments are often influenced by self-interest.

d. participants are more likely to endorse a claim if it is consistent with beliefs the participants had to begin with.

Answer: a

40. The text gives an example that juxtaposes Alan's claim that he has a great method for choosing lottery numbers because he used it and won once, and Lila's claim that she has a great method that has worked for her 11 times. This example shows that:

a. people will never use statistical knowledge without cues to do so.

b. people understand the risk associated with buying lottery tickets.

c. people's judgments are too often based on the opinions of others.

d. people understand that accidents happen, but don't keep happening.

Answer: d

41. Evolutionary psychologists argue that because of environmental conditions many, many years ago, humans are better able to make judgments based on information presented as _____ than as _____.

a. percentages; fractions

b. abstract ideas; concrete examples

c. frequencies; probabilities

d. probabilities; frequencies

Answer: c

42. The "law of large numbers" implies that larger samples of data are less likely to show accidental patterns; therefore, larger samples are generally more informative. In making judgments about evidence:

a. participants seem to understand and respect the principle.

b. participants ignore the principle even though they do follow other principles of statistics.

c. participants follow the principle only if they have been trained in statistics.

d. participants ignore the principle in some situations but respect it in other situations.

Answer: d

43. Nisbett has argued that participants do understand the basic principles of statistics but often fail to use their knowledge. Which of the following situations does *not* contain one of the triggers that leads to the use of statistical knowledge?

a. The role of chance or accident is prominent in the problem under scrutiny.

b. The participant is scrutinizing a problem that is of great personal importance, so the participant is highly motivated to reason carefully and well.

   c. The problem under scrutiny makes clear that the available evidence is a sample of data, drawn from a larger set of potential observations.

   d. The problem being considered involves a situation for which the participant has background beliefs emphasizing the role of luck or chance.

Answer: b

44. Studies indicate that training in statistics:
   a. has little impact on how participants make judgments outside of the statistics class.
   b. improves participants' understanding of statistical principles but does not teach them how to apply the principles to actual cases.
   c. helps participants make more accurate judgments, but only if the participants were explicitly encouraged to apply their statistical knowledge.
   d. improves participants' performance in a variety of judgment problems.

Answer: d

45. An undergraduate education:
   a. improves participants' ability to make judgments, and the benefit is particularly large for students who majored in psychology and social science.
   b. improves participants' ability to make judgments, but only if the student majored in mathematics or some other discipline involving much work in mathematics.
   c. improves participants' ability to make judgments in a fashion virtually independent of the student's major.
   d. provides many benefits, but seems not to teach students how to make more accurate judgments.

Answer: a

CHAPTER 13 | Reasoning: Thinking Through the Implications of What You Know

1. "Deduction" is a process that:
   a. allows us to extrapolate from a sample of evidence.
   b. allows us to make specific predictions based on more general knowledge.
   c. helps us to draw general conclusions based on specific facts.
   d. helps us to determine if a pattern exists in a set of observations.

   Answer: b

2. Isaac Newton's theories make a huge number of predictions, and the evidence generally fits with the predictions. Nonetheless, most physicists believe that Newton's theories are wrong. This state of affairs highlights the ambiguity of:
   a. normative data.
   b. disconfirmation.
   c. confirming evidence.
   d. hypothesis testing.

   Answer: c

3. Which of the following is *not* an aspect of confirmation bias?
   a. People seek evidence that is likely to fit with their beliefs, rather than evidence that might challenge their beliefs.
   b. People fail to adjust their beliefs when they encounter facts that are inconsistent with those beliefs.
   c. People often fail to consider alternative hypotheses that might explain the available data just as well as the current hypothesis does.
   d. People seem to have better recollection for evidence inconsistent with their beliefs than for evidence that is consistent.

   Answer: d

4. Participants were presented with a group of numbers, such as "2, 4, 6," and were told that the numbers followed a certain rule. The participants' task was to determine the rule. Sam's hypothesis is this: "The second number must be two higher than the first, and the third number must be two higher than the second." To test his hypothesis, Sam asks the experimenter, "Does 14, 16, 18 fit with the rule?" Sam's question:
   a. is consistent with the pattern called confirmation bias.
   b. is contrary to the pattern called confirmation bias.
   c. may or may not reveal confirmation bias, depending on what the rule actually is.
   d. may or may not reveal confirmation bias, depending on how the experimenter answers.

   Answer: a

5. Participants in an experiment were told that they were particularly good at a task requiring social skills. Later, they were told that this information was utterly bogus, and they were told that all participants had received the same feedback. Then, at the end of the experiment, the participants were asked just how good they thought their social skills really were. Based on other studies, we should predict that, in this final self-assessment, participants:
   a. will show a strong contrast effect, thereby underestimating their social skills.
   b. will continue to believe the information they initially received, thereby overestimating their social skills.
   c. will be unable to integrate the sequence of inputs and will end up uncertain of how to assess their social skills.
   d. will rely on their bias toward trusting recent information and will be able to disregard the initial (bogus) feedback.

   Answer: b

6. Belief perseverance is one of the phenomena used to demonstrate:
   a. normative thinking.
   b. confirmation bias.
   c. rigid thinking.
   d. nonselective memory search.

   Answer: b

7. A friend says to Henry, "You tend to be more reflective than the people around you." Henry is initially uncertain about whether or not this is true, and to find out, he is likely to search through memory:
   a. looking for prior episodes in which he was reflective.
   b. looking for prior episodes in which he failed to be reflective.

   c. looking for prior episodes in which he was reflective and for ones in which he was not.

   d. looking for any information at all that might bear on this suggestion.

Answer: a

8. In tests of logic, participants make huge numbers of errors, and the errors fall into systematic patterns. This is *inconsistent* with the claim that thought:
   a. relies heavily on pragmatic reasoning schemata.
   b. regularly makes use of categorical syllogisms.
   c. proceeds according to the standard rules of logic, so reasoning errors are likely to be the result of carelessness.
   d. follows rules of "natural logic," different from the standard rules proposed by mathematicians and logicians.

Answer: c

9. "All television shows are junk. Junk is not worth watching. Therefore, all television shows are not worth watching." This is an example of:
   a. conditional reasoning.
   b. a categorical syllogism.
   c. modus ponens.
   d. induction.

Answer: b

10. Participants are more likely to judge a syllogism to be valid if:
    a. the syllogism is phrased in abstract terms.
    b. the conclusion contains the word "all."
    c. the conclusion is a statement participants believe to be true based on other knowledge.
    d. the participants have been trained in logic.

Answer: c

11. The term _____ refers to a tendency to affirm a conclusion that contains the word "all" if both premises contain the word "all."
    a. belief perseverance
    b. belief bias
    c. conversion error
    d. atmosphere effect

Answer: d

12. Which of the following claims is *false*?
    a. Participants interpret "All A are B" as if it also meant "All B are A."
    b. If the premises of a syllogism contain the word "not," participants are likely to endorse a conclusion containing "not."

    c. Participants are influenced by whether or not the conclusion of a syllogism fits with other things they believe.

    d. Participants tend to reject conclusions based on abstract premises.

Answer: d

13. The notion of a "natural logic" implies all of the following *except*:

    a. participants' understanding of terms like "if" and "or" may be different from the way these terms are understood in standard logic.

    b. participants' reasoning proceeds in concrete terms as participants draw analogies from familiar cases.

    c. participants' understanding of logic may not include some rules, such as modus tollens.

    d. participants' reasoning may follow legitimate rules, but rules that are different from those endorsed by logicians.

Answer: b

14. "If P is true, then Q must be true. Q is not true. Therefore, P must not be true." This states:

    a. the rule called modus tollens.

    b. the rule called modus ponens.

    c. an invalid conclusion.

    d. a categorical syllogism.

Answer: a

15. Participants are shown four cards, and each card has a word or symbol on each side. Participants are asked which cards they would need to turn over in order to test a certain rule. Participants' performance will be:

    a. poor unless the rule contains a situation with which the participants are already familiar.

    b. poor unless the rule is framed in concrete terms.

    c. good if the participants perceive a rationale for the rule.

    d. good if the rule involves modus tollens.

Answer: c

16. Part of the reason that participants have difficulty with the four-card problem is likely to be that:

    a. abstract logical thinking is always difficult for participants.

    b. modus tollens is not natural for most participants, although modus ponens is.

    c. modus ponens is not natural for most participants, although modus tollens is.

    d. they are better at solving problems based on conditional statements than on categorical syllogisms.

Answer: b

17. According to an evolutionary psychological perspective, people will perform better on a reasoning problem if that problem can be related to:
    a. hunting or gathering.
    b. permission.
    c. detecting cheaters or betrayal.
    d. statements about necessity rather than sufficiency.

    Answer: c

18. Which of the following claims is *false*?
    a. Pragmatic reasoning schemata are more abstract than logical rules.
    b. Pragmatic reasoning schemata are derived from the redundant patterns in our experiences.
    c. Pragmatic reasoning schemata are defined in terms of goals or event relationships.
    d. Pragmatic reasoning schemata involve rules that often lead to the same conclusions as do the rules of logic.

    Answer: a

19. Participants are told, "If a person wishes to drink alcohol, the person must be over 21 years old." Participants are then asked which cases they would need to investigate in order to determine if the rule is being followed. Given the available evidence, we should expect that participants will reason:
    a. well in testing this rule because it involves the relatively familiar rule of modus ponens.
    b. well in testing this rule because it is likely to be understood in terms of permission.
    c. poorly with this rule because testing the rule requires the use of modus tollens.
    d. poorly with this rule because they are likely to blur the rule together with other similar cases they have encountered.

    Answer: b

20. Pragmatic reasoning schemata help participants to reason only if:
    a. the problem involves familiar materials.
    b. the problem triggers one of the schemata, such as permission or obligation.
    c. the problem is phrased in concrete terms.
    d. the problem involves a cause-and-effect relationship.

    Answer: b

21. One theoretical account of the original (number and letter) version of the four-card problem states that:
    a. the uniformly poor performance on this task suggests that participants are reading it as a question of sufficiency.

b. the uniformly poor performance on this task suggests that participants are reading it as a question of necessity.

c. the varied results reflect the fact that this task is ambiguous with respect to necessity and sufficiency rules.

d. performance on this task suggests that it cannot be cast in terms of necessity or sufficiency rules.

Answer: c

22. A researcher tests participants on the "four-card" (or "selection") problem. On this problem, students who have taken a college course in logic:

a. perform at a higher level.

b. perform at a higher level, but only if the problem is framed in abstract terms.

c. perform at a higher level if the problem's phrasing contains triggers for their logic knowledge.

d. perform at the same level as participants who have received no training in logic.

Answer: d

23. Participants were first trained to use reasoning schemata and were then tested with various versions of the "four-card" (or "selection") problem. The results showed that training:

a. had no impact on participants' performance.

b. improved participants' performance.

c. improved the participants' ability to use formal logic.

d. improved participants' performance, but only if the problem was phrased in terms of a familiar case.

Answer: b

24. Which of the following claims about deductive logic is *false*?

a. Subjects can learn to reason in a fashion governed by the laws of formal logic.

b. Each subject seems to have a preferred way of approaching all reasoning problems.

c. If a problem triggers a reasoning schema, subjects will reason in a fashion guided by the schema.

d. People reason more effectively with abstract materials than with concrete materials.

Answer: b

25. Compared to college courses in statistics, college courses in logic:

a. seem to have a smaller impact on participants' informal reasoning.

b. seem to build on a set of intuitions participants already held before taking the course.

c. seem to have a larger impact on participants' informal reasoning.

d. have an impact on participants' reasoning only if the courses emphasize general rules and principles rather than specific examples.

Answer: a

26. The text argues that a full account of human reasoning requires a minimum of three layers: First, in some situations people can use formal or "natural" logic. Second, people use complex strategies including pragmatic reasoning schemata. Third:
    a. evolutionary considerations must be taken into account.
    b. problems must be translated into abstract terms so that formal logic can be used.
    c. multiple levels of mental models must be used.
    d. when these other strategies are not triggered, people rely on outside information or a problem's phrasing.

Answer: d

27. Which of the follow claims about mental models is *false*?
    a. Mental models translate abstract information into a relatively concrete presentation.
    b. Participants are able to scrutinize a mental model in order to discover what conclusions follow from the modeled situation.
    c. Each logical statement is compatible with just a single mental model.
    d. It requires some effort to maintain multiple models simultaneously.

Answer: c

28. Which of the following observations would be *inconsistent* with the claim that participants often use mental models to guide their reasoning?
    a. The greater the number of models needed to reason through a problem, the more likely errors are to occur.
    b. Participants' self-reports often indicate a reliance on mental models.
    c. Participants' performance improves if the premises of a problem are presented in a sequence that decreases the number of mental models needed to solve the problem.
    d. If a problem's premises can be modeled in many different ways, the problem will be easier to solve.

Answer: d

29. In theories of decision making, "utility" of a particular commodity can be defined in terms of:
    a. the degree of value associated with the commodity for a social group.
    b. the value that has historically been placed on the commodity.
    c. the monetary cost associated with the commodity.
    d. the subjective value associated with the commodity for each individual.

Answer: d

30. The "expected utility" associated with an action:
    a. provides an estimate that is independent of the likelihood of reaching the action's desired outcome.
    b. can be calculated as a value independent of the action's consequences.
    c. is calculated as the utility of the likely outcome of the action multiplied by the probability of reaching that outcome.
    d. is negative if the likelihood of success with the action is extremely low.

Answer: c

31. Research on decision making indicates that participants:
    a. consistently seek to maximize expected utility.
    b. make choices guided by a strong tendency toward consistency with previous choices.
    c. show inconsistencies in their choices that follow no systematic pattern.
    d. are heavily influenced by minor changes in a problem's wording.

Answer: d

32. When researchers speak of a decision's "frame," they are referring to:
    a. changes in one's assumptions about a decision that have the impact of altering the expected utility of that decision.
    b. aspects of how the decision is phrased that are irrelevant to the utility of the decision.
    c. the pattern of needs and values that a participant brings to each decision.
    d. aspects of how a question is worded that have no impact on the participant's decisions about that question.

Answer: b

33. Of the following, the greatest concern associated with "framing effects" is that:
    a. frames can lead participants to make risk-seeking decisions.
    b. frames can lead participants to make risk-averse decisions.
    c. frames can lead participants to ignore factors that are clearly pertinent to their decision.
    d. changes in a decision's frame can lead participants to contradict themselves.

Answer: d

34. Which of the following is *not* a serious problem for the regular use of utility theory?
    a. People are heavily swayed by how a decision is phrased, even if the phrasing has no impact on utilities.
    b. People have no idea how to perform the calculations required for this theory.
    c. People's values tend to fluctuate depending on context.
    d. People have difficulty labeling benefits and costs.

Answer: b

35. Research on framing effects demonstrates that people who are considering potential losses are likely to:
    a. accept courses of action that contain an element of risk.
    b. minimize their degree of risk.
    c. choose options that are highly conservative.
    d. seek paths that will maximize their utility.

    Answer: a

36. Mimi rarely takes chances because she hates the idea of losing. It sounds like Mimi is being:
    a. persuaded by a sunk cost.
    b. influenced by framing.
    c. risk averse.
    d. risk seeking.

    Answer: c

37. Which of the following is plainly *not* consistent with utility maximization?
    a. being risk seeking
    b. being risk averse
    c. being influenced by a sunk cost.
    d. being conservative in the face of risk

    Answer: c

38. If a decision is too complicated, the participant may try to simplify the decision by:
    a. framing the decision in terms of a gain rather than in terms of a loss.
    b. considering the options in a step-by-step fashion, focusing on just one attribute at a time.
    c. seeking to optimize rather than to satisfice.
    d. focusing on the certain outcomes rather than on the risky outcomes.

    Answer: b

39. Participants tend to be:
    a. more sensitive to gains than to corresponding losses.
    b. more sensitive to losses than to corresponding gains.
    c. equally sensitive to losses and gains.
    d. unreliable in how they evaluate losses and gains.

    Answer: b

40. Participants' great sensitivity to losses is evident in all of the following *except*:
    a. Participants will often take risky courses of action in hopes of avoiding a loss.
    b. When confronting a potential loss, participants will avoid any gambles, to make certain they don't lose any more than necessary.

c. Participants tend to overvalue the things they own, placing a higher value on those objects than they would if the same object were owned by someone else.

d. In making decisions, participants place greater weight on the disadvantages associated with a course of action than on the advantages.

Answer: b

41. "Let's toss a coin. If it comes up heads, I'll pay you $5. If it comes up "tails," you pay me $5." Participants generally refuse to play this game, probably because:
    a. they are sensitive to the pattern of expected utility.
    b. they fail to understand the relevant probabilities.
    c. the prospect of losing $5 seems more consequential than the prospect of winning $5, so the bet seems unfair.
    d. participants realize that this is an even bet, with no real potential for gain.

Answer: c

42. The term "sunk cost" refers to:
    a. a cost that has already occurred and is now irreversible.
    b. an initial down payment that serves to commit someone to a decision.
    c. the cost that derives from losing a gamble.
    d. how participants perceive a cost prior to actually paying the cost.

Answer: a

43. According to utility theory, one should:
    a. be sensitive to sunk cost to make certain that one's initial investment is not wasted.
    b. anticipate sunk costs when choosing among any set of options.
    c. disregard sunk costs because the cost is not reclaimable, no matter what action one takes.
    d. count sunk costs as a disutility in any calculation of utilities.

Answer: c

44. Theorists have proposed a model of decision making based on reasons rather than on the calculation of utilities. Their proposal is that participants decide to take one option rather than another only when:
    a. the expected utility of the option is clearly greater than the expected utility of any other option.
    b. the choice fits socially defined norms.
    c. they see a compelling argument for making that choice.
    d. the decision is framed in terms of gains rather than losses.

Answer: c

45. Steve goes to the store to buy a radio. The store has two different models available, both of very good quality and at reasonable prices. Nevertheless, Steve ends up buying neither. Given what we know about decision making, the most promising explanation is that Steve:
    a. couldn't find a persuasive reason for buying one radio rather than the other, so he bought neither.
    b. changed his mind in the store and decided he didn't want a radio after all.
    c. calculated the expected utility of further shopping and decided that that was his best option.
    d. realized that the utility of each radio was lower than its purchase price, making the radios unappealing.

    Answer: a

46. The text suggests that utility theory, while not a very good _____ theory of people's reasoning, may none the less be a good _____ theory.
    a. productive; inductive
    b. normative; descriptive
    c. inductive; productive
    d. descriptive; normative

    Answer: d

CHAPTER 14 | Solving Problems

1. Some psychologists describe problem solving as a process of "search." Which of the following is *not* part of this description?
   a. the problem's "initial state"
   b. the problem's "path conflicts"
   c. the problem's "goal state"
   d. the problem's "operators"

   Answer: b

2. A problem's "initial state" refers to:
   a. the participant's circumstances before he or she has understood the problem.
   b. the actual statement of the problem.
   c. the knowledge and resources one possesses at the outset of the problem.
   d. the first goal one must move toward in solving the problem.

   Answer: c

3. All of the states one can reach in solving a problem together make up the:
   a. operators.
   b. pathways.
   c. problem definition.
   d. problem space.

   Answer: d

4. One plan for solving a problem would be to consider every possible option, searching for the best solution. This broad plan:
   a. is usually the best way to proceed for complicated problems.
   b. is more effective with ill-defined problems.

c. is usually ruled out by the sheer number of possible states within the problem space.

d. is often the only plan available.

Answer: c

5. A problem-solving heuristic:
    a. is guaranteed to find a problem solution, if one exists.
    b. is a strategy that guides a search through the problem space.
    c. is likely to be less effective than a strategy such as hill climbing or means-end analysis.
    d. is needed for unfamiliar problems, but not for familiar problems.

Answer: b

6. "Problem-solving protocols" are:
    a. moment-by-moment records of what participants say when asked to think aloud while working on a problem.
    b. the output from computer models programmed to simulate human problem solving.
    c. procedures designed by problem-solving experts.
    d. reports by the participant, after the problem has been solved, about which strategies seemed useful and which seemed unproductive.

Answer: a

7. Participants' use of "hill climbing" is evident in that:
    a. participants solve problems more quickly if they can divide the problem into smaller subproblems.
    b. problem solving often gets stalled if a problem requires the participant to move briefly away from the goal state in order (ultimately) to reach the goal.
    c. participants are disrupted in their problem solving if they are asked to think out loud as they proceed.
    d. participants are often confused unless the problem's path constraints are clearly specified.

Answer: b

8. Which of the following is *not* a heuristic used in problem solving?
    a. framing
    b. hill-climbing
    c. means-end analysis
    d. working backward from the goal state

Answer: a

9. Which of the following is *not* an advantage gained by visualizing a problem via a mental image?
   a. The image depicts the problem in a concrete way, and this often makes the problem easier to remember.
   b. The image often makes it easy to discern how the elements of the problem are related to one another.
   c. One can easily make new discoveries about the imaged form, including discoveries that involve an entirely new understanding of the form.
   d. It is usually easy to rearrange the elements of an image to explore other configurations.

   Answer: c

10. A number of researchers have programmed computers to solve problems in the same ways that humans do. This computer modeling has been moderately successful so far, and the success is evident in all of the following *except*:
    a. the computer models are able to solve many of the problems that humans solve.
    b. the computers seem to have difficulty with roughly the same problems that humans do.
    c. the step-by-step operations of the computer model correspond reasonably well with the steps revealed in participants' problem solving protocols.
    d. the researchers have been able to program the computers to approach problems in a creative and novel fashion.

    Answer: d

11. Computer models of problem solving have all of the following features *except*:
    a. these models often rely on heuristics such as means-end analysis.
    b. these models often rely on production systems as their operators.
    c. these models proceed more slowly when they must consider numerous subgoals.
    d. these models employ distributed processing to compensate if the programmer has provided vague or ambiguous instructions.

    Answer: d

12. Analogies are:
    a. often misleading, since an analogy, by its nature, depends on a problem's surface structure.
    b. relatively ineffective for solving problems, unless the problem is a familiar one.
    c. an effective way to promote understanding and problem solving.
    d. relevant only for a narrow set of problems.

    Answer: c

13. Studies of analogy use indicate that participants:
    a. use analogies spontaneously in a wide range of problems.
    b. use analogies only if they are experts in the domain of the problem.
    c. are more likely to use analogies if there is a superficial resemblance between the problem being solved and the problem serving as the base for the analogy.
    d. are more likely to use analogies in solving spatial problems than they are in solving verbal problems.

    Answer: c

14. Dell is trying to solve the "hobbits and orcs" problem, so she must determine how to move the creatures across a river. Dell is most likely to be helped if she has had earlier experience with:
    a. a similar problem also involving hobbits and orcs.
    b. a formally identical problem involving jealous husbands and their wives.
    c. other problems involving transportation across obstacles.
    d. problems illustrating the techniques for dealing with river currents.

    Answer: a

15. In many studies, participants fail to use analogies as an aid to problem solving. Of the following, which is the most plausible explanation of this fact?
    a. Participants don't understand the value of analogies, so they don't bother searching for them.
    b. Participants search their memories by asking, "What else do I know about problems on this topic?" As a result, they fail to think of analogous cases that happen to be concerned with a different topic.
    c. Participants pay too much attention to the deep structure of a problem, and so they fail to see the features that lead to analogy.
    d. Participants seem unable to use analogies even when explicitly instructed to do so.

    Answer: b

16. Herbert solved the "tumor" problem by using an analogy with the "general and fortress" problem. In doing this, he realized that "tumor" corresponds to "fortress," "radiation" corresponds to "attacking army," and so on. The process of determining these correspondences is called:
    a. translating.
    b. analogizing.
    c. mapping.
    d. parsing.

    Answer: c

17. A participant was given practice in solving the "jealous husbands" problem and was then tested with the "hobbits and orcs" problem. The participant, however, was unable to figure out how to map the problems onto one another. This is evident in the fact that:
    a. in solving the "hobbits" problem, the participant asked herself, "What else do I know about hobbits?"
    b. the participant was unpersuaded that an analogy would be helpful.
    c. the participant was unable to think of an analogous case even though she tried to do so.
    d. the participant didn't realize that the rule "Orcs can not outnumber hobbits" corresponds to the rule "Husbands can not be left alone with other men's wives."

    Answer: d

18. Which of the following is *not* a procedure that makes analogy use more likely?
    a. Participants are given two analogous problems, rather than just one, before the test problem.
    b. Participants are given financial bonuses for each one of the test problems they are able to solve.
    c. Participants are given several training problems and asked to compare the problems to one another.
    d. Participants are encouraged to work at understanding the solutions of the training problems so that they can explain the solutions later on.

    Answer: b

19. In general, a training procedure will promote subsequent analogy use if the procedure:
    a. helps participants to remember the exact formulation of the training problems.
    b. makes the value of analogy use clear to participants.
    c. encourages participants to pay attention to the training problem's deep structure.
    d. teaches the participants general principles about how analogies function.

    Answer: c

20. In order to teach students to be better problem solvers, we should do all of the following *except*:
    a. teach some of the general-purpose heuristics, such as means-end analysis or working backward.
    b. teach them to pay better attention to problem solving protocols.
    c. provide students with experience in the relevant domains so that they will have a basis from which to draw analogies.
    d. encourage students to approach their training with attention to deep structure rather than to surface details.

    Answer: b

21. Expert problem solvers:
    a. focus on the surface of a problem rather than on its deep structure.
    b. use analogies less often than do novices.
    c. tend to categorize problems in terms of their deep structure.
    d. do not need to rely on mapping in their use of analogies.

    Answer: c

22. Compared to novices, chess experts have:
    a. better memory for the positions of pieces on a chess board, but only if the pieces are arranged in a fashion that respects the rules of chess.
    b. better memory for the positions of pieces on a chess board, no matter how the pieces are arranged.
    c. better visual memories in general.
    d. no memory advantage.

    Answer: a

23. Experts seem able to break a problem into meaningful chunks. This strategy provides all of the following advantages *except*:
    a. it makes it easier to remember the various elements of the problem.
    b. it highlights the organization of the problem's elements, making it easier to see the problem's structure.
    c. it helps in the identification of subproblems and therefore in the creation of subgoals.
    d. it draws the expert's attention to the problem's microstructure.

    Answer: d

24. People often compare experts to novices. Which of the following claims about this comparison is *false*?
    a. Experts tend to be more skilled problem solvers in general, so they have an advantage with problems of all sorts.
    b. Experts have a much larger knowledge base, including a large set of exemplars on which they can draw.
    c. Experts are more familiar with the higher-order patterns common in the area of expertise.
    d. Expert knowledge is more heavily "cross-referenced" and is therefore more easily accessible.

    Answer: a

25. The "working backward" strategy:
    a. is virtually never used by experts.
    b. is used by experts if they are working on an unfamiliar problem.
    c. is used far more often by experts than by novices.
    d. is used in the same way by experts and by novices.

    Answer: b

26. Which of the following problems is ill defined?
    a. Sarah is trying to think of a way to impress her boss.
    b. Susan is trying to decide which route to take to the soccer game.
    c. Sheila can't decide whether to go to a movie this evening or to study in the library.
    d. Samantha is having trouble choosing which courses to take next semester.

    Answer: a

27. An ill-defined problem is defined as one in which:
    a. there is more than one path available that will lead to the goal.
    b. the problem does not have clearly defined subgoals.
    c. neither analogies nor heuristics will lead to a problem solution.
    d. there is initially some uncertainty about what operators are available and what path constraints are in place.

    Answer: d

28. The tendency to be rigid in how one thinks about an object's function is called:
    a. mental stickiness.
    b. functional fixedness.
    c. functional narrowness.
    d. narrow focus.

    Answer: b

29. It was starting to rain, and Marcus didn't have an umbrella or a hat. To keep dry, he held his psychology textbook over his head. In this case, Marcus:
    a. is showing the influence of Einstellung.
    b. has solved the problem by using functional fixedness.
    c. has managed to overcome functional fixedness.
    d. is making the best possible use of his textbook.

    Answer: c

30. In solving a problem, participants seem to develop a certain attitude or perspective, and they then approach all subsequent problems with the same rigid attitude. This rigidity in approach is often called:
    a. transfer.
    b. Einstellung.
    c. mental inhibition.
    d. Zeitgeist.

    Answer: b

31. A group of participants has just completed a series of problems involving water jars. In each problem, the participants needed to fill the largest jar, pour from it once into the middle-sized jar, and then pour from the largest

jar twice into the smallest jar. The participants are now given a new problem, which can not be solved via this procedure. We would expect that:
a. the participants will quickly solve the new problem because they have had practice with a series of very similar problems.
b. the participants will be unable to solve the new problem because they are now locked in to the procedure they had used successfully.
c. the participants will behave just like participants who have no experience with water jar problems; that is, there will be no effect of the prior training.
d. the participants will try their already practiced procedure and, once they realize this procedure does not help them, they will show no effect of the prior training.

Answer: b

32. Participants approach a problem with certain assumptions about how the problem should be handled and the sorts of strategies that are likely to be productive. These assumptions are referred to as:
a. functional fixedness.
b. well definedness.
c. a problem frame.
d. a problem solving set.

Answer: d

33. A problem solving set:
a. is generally a deterrent to problem solving, so one should seek to approach a problem without a set.
b. is an obstacle for novice problem solvers, but not for experts.
c. is crucial for well-defined problems but can not help with ill-defined problems.
d. often helps because the set leads us ignore a number of options that obviously will not lead to the goal.

Answer: d

34. In general, the technique known as "brainstorming":
a. increases the quantity, but not the quality, of ideas produced.
b. increases the quality, but not the quantity, of ideas produced.
c. increases both the quality and the quantity of ideas produced.
d. has no effect on either the quantity or the quality of ideas produced.

Answer: a

35. Psychologists interested in creativity:
a. insist that creativity can not be defined.
b. define a creative discovery as one that is novel and also useful or valuable.

   c. argue that creativity can not be measured.

   d. have equated creativity with intelligence.

Answer: b

36. Some scholars have argued that "divergent thinking" plays a central role in creativity. This is a form of thinking in which:

   a. one considers an idea from two perspectives at the same time.

   b. one develops ideas in a new and unprecedented direction.

   c. one pursues an idea by setting aside some of the themes often associated with the idea.

   d. one gradually brings an idea closer and closer to the creative goal.

Answer: b

37. Mednick designed the Remote Associates Test (RAT) to measure creativity; this test assumes that a key element of creativity is:

   a. the ability to remain flexible in one's approach to an idea.

   b. the ability to tolerate ambiguity, especially in the early stages of a project.

   c. the ability to explore unanticipated consequences of familiar ideas.

   d. the ability to find new connections among ideas.

Answer: d

38. Much of what we know about creativity comes from case studies of enormously creative individuals, with the evidence often coming from the individuals themselves. Which of the following is the *least* troubling about the interpretation of the case studies?

   a. The reports were often recorded years after the creative event.

   b. Many of the reports involve discoveries that were not considered creative at the time the discovery occurred.

   c. The creative individuals may have adjusted the facts to present themselves in a favorable light.

   d. Creative discoveries often rely on nonverbal thoughts, and it is therefore unclear whether or not a creative discovery can be accurately represented in a verbal report.

Answer: b

39. Many years ago, Wallas argued that creative thought proceeds through four stages; which of the following is *not* one of these stages?

   a. illumination

   b. articulation

   c. preparation

   d. incubation

Answer: b

40. As Vanessa worked on the problem, she reported out loud, "No, that option seems not to work. No, that doesn't work either." Then Vanessa abruptly shouted, "I think I've got it!" These reports seem to capture the phenomenon called:
   a. illumination.
   b. incubation.
   c. preparation.
   d. representation.

   Answer: a

41. Researchers have tried to study the "moment of illumination" in the laboratory. The evidence indicates that:
   a. this experience can not be observed reliably in laboratory conditions.
   b. there is no systematic relationship between reports of illumination and actual progress in problem solving.
   c. when participants report an illumination, they are at least as likely to be moving toward a dead end as they are to be moving toward the problem's solution.
   d. when participants report an illumination, they have in fact made a discovery that will allow them to solve the problem.

   Answer: c

42. A group of participants is interrupted while working on a problem. The participants then spend some time on an unrelated task, and, finally, they return to the initial problem. Studies of this sort show that:
   a. the participants will benefit from the interruption and are more likely to solve the problem when they return to it.
   b. the participants will be disrupted by the interruption and are less likely to solve the problem when they return to it.
   c. the participants will not be affected by the interruption.
   d. the data are mixed, with some studies showing a benefit from the interruption but with many studies showing no effect.

   Answer: d

43. In some procedures, participants are helped by an interruption during their attempts at solving a problem. In explaining this effect, which of the following hypotheses seems *least* plausible in light of the available evidence?
   a. The interruption provides an opportunity for participants to gather further information about the problem.
   b. The interruption provides an opportunity for frustration or fatigue to dissipate.

  c. The interruption allows participants to forget their earlier approaches to the problem, thus enabling a fresh start.

  d. The interruption allows an opportunity for unconscious problem solving to occur.

Answer: d

44. According to the text, current research indicates that creative problem solving:

  a. draws on mental processes that are distinct from the processes relevant to more ordinary problem solving.

  b. depends on divergent thinking.

  c. draws on heuristics and analogies in the same way as does ordinary problem solving.

  d. requires unconscious work that goes on after one has consciously put the problem to the side.

Answer: c

| Conscious Thought,
Unconscious Thought

1. In the late 1800s the young science of psychology:
   a. considered consciousness to be a central concern of the science.
   b. argued that consciousness could not be studied scientifically.
   c. studied consciousness by focusing on the biological roots of conscious thought.
   d. largely ignored the topic of consciousness.

   Answer: a

2. The text argues that much of our current understanding of consciousness derives from:
   a. advances in our ability to scrutinize the details of brain functioning.
   b. studies of what can be done in the absence of consciousness.
   c. chronometric studies.
   d. an increased sophistication in our ability to analyze introspective reports.

   Answer: b

3. A great deal of "behind the scenes" activity is necessary to make possible intellectual achievements like thinking and remembering. This "behind the scenes" activity is referred to by psychologists as:
   a. "nuts and bolts work."
   b. "the cognitive unconscious."
   c. "subconscious production."
   d. "running program."

   Answer: b

4. Several authors have proposed that we are generally aware of the _____ of our own thoughts even though we are usually unaware of the _____ of thought:

a. product; processes
b. decision making processes; products
c. implicit mechanisms; explicit mechanisms
d. inferences; strategies

Answer: a

5. Which of the following is not an example of the principle "We are aware of products, but not of processes"?
   a. Jeff knew that the stimulus seemed familiar, but he didn't know why.
   b. Jesse believed that the stimulus was "cake," but he couldn't tell whether he'd seen the stimulus or just inferred it.
   c. Jeremy suddenly found himself thinking about marriage, and he couldn't figure out what had brought this idea into his thoughts.
   d. Jacob wanted to do well on the spelling test, but he didn't know the best way to study the words.

Answer: d

6. Our unconscious thinking about an event:
   a. tends to be simple and direct, leading us, for example, to think of the event as "familiar," or "preferable."
   b. can often be quite complex, involving several steps of reasoning and inference.
   c. can influence us in small ways but seems not to have larger-scale impact.
   d. is most influential with novel events; with familiar events, we react in a more reflective fashion.

Answer: b

7. In one study, participants in Group 1 were given a pill and were told, "This pill will make you a bit jumpy, will make your palms sweat, and may give you butterflies in the stomach." Participants in Group 2 were given the same pill, but they were told, "This pill may make you a little sleepy." In both cases, the pill was a placebo. All participants were then exposed to electric shocks and were asked to rate how painful each shock had seemed. Given other evidence, we should expect that:
   a. there will be no difference between the two groups.
   b. the participants will not differ in how they rate the shocks, but participants in Group 2 will end up having more positive feelings about the experiment.
   c. participants in Group 2 will rate the shocks as less painful than participants in Group 1.
   d. participants in Group 1 will rate the shocks as less painful than participants in Group 2.

Answer: d

8. Sometimes we reason carefully and deliberately through an argument, scrutinizing each step. In this sort of case:
   a. our thoughts will be entirely conscious even if we are unconscious of our thoughts in other situations.
   b. the processes of our thoughts, but not the products, will be consciously available.
   c. our sequence of thoughts depends on an unconscious support structure that guides how we interpret the elements of each thought.
   d. we are engaging in schema-based reasoning.

   Answer: c

9. Solomon thought to himself, "I must stay away from the bank." According to the text:
   a. Solomon was probably uncertain whether he was thinking about a river's edge or a financial institution.
   b. this thought would be ambiguous by itself, but subsequent thoughts remove the ambiguity.
   c. Solomon's thought is clear and well defined and refers to both a river's edge and a financial institution.
   d. the ambiguity of this thought is resolved by the unconscious support structure that seems to provide a context for all thought.

   Answer: d

10. Our thoughts seem to be embedded in a context that is usually not noticed, but the context serves to define and guide the thoughts. Which of the following is not an example of this sort of context?
    a. Discovery based on mental imagery is influenced by the perceptual reference frame for the image.
    b. Decisions are guided by how the decision is framed.
    c. The meaning of the terms involved in our thoughts is clarified by the surrounding context of thought.
    d. Perception of a word or object is strongly shaped by the other words and objects that surround the target.

    Answer: d

11. Spelke, Hirst, and Neisser trained their participants to read a book while simultaneously taking dictation. Their data indicate that:
    a. participants were able to write down the dictated material but were unable to remember the material later on.
    b. participants were able to write down the dictated material but were unable to comprehend what the "unattended" material meant.

    c. participants were unaware of what they had accomplished, so they did
not realize that they had actually understood the dictated material.

    d. participants were fully aware of the meaning of both the material they
were reading and the dictated material.

Answer: c

12. Patients with Korsakoff's amnesia seem to:

    a. be capable of learning even though they do poorly in explicit tests of
memory.

    b. remember virtually nothing of the events occurring subsequent to the
onset of their illness.

    c. perform well on tests requiring conscious recollection even though their
performance is poor if memory is tested indirectly.

    d. be unable to recall material learned in the past even though they recognize
the material when they encounter it.

Answer: a

13. The phrase "memory without awareness" is another way of describing a
pattern in which:

    a. explicit memory tests indicate that a participant remembers an event, but
implicit memory tests indicate that the participant does not remember.

    b. implicit memory tests indicate that a participant remembers an event, but
explicit memory tests indicate that the participant does not remember.

    c. recognition tests indicate that a participant remembers an event, but
recall tests indicate that the participant does not remember.

    d. direct memory testing indicates that a participant remembers an event,
but indirect testing indicates that the participant does not remember.

Answer: b

14. A patient with blind-sight is likely to show all of the following traits except:

    a. if asked to walk across the room the patient does so easily.

    b. if asked to reach toward an object, the patient tends to reach in the
appropriate direction.

    c. if asked to reach toward an object, the patient tends to reach with the
appropriate hand position (e.g., hand wide open if the target is large).

    d. if asked to guess the identity of a visual stimulus, the patient's guesses
are consistently correct.

Answer: a

15. Data based solely on introspection can be problematic for all of the following
reasons, *except*:

    a. much of mental processing is invisible to introspection.

    b. self-report is generally based on memory.

    c. participants are usually resistant to providing self-report data.

    d. introspection self-report may lack sincerity.

Answer: c

16. There are many reasons why introspection is a poor source of scientific evidence. Which of the following is *not* one of those reasons?
    a. Many mental events are too quick for introspection.
    b. Participants must be carefully trained before they are able to introspect effectively.
    c. Participants' reports are based on memory and are therefore vulnerable to error.
    d. Participants' reports may in some cases be insincere.

Answer: b

17. Two participants both report that they have extremely vivid visual imagery. This report:
    a. is difficult to interpret, since we have no way of knowing whether the two participants mean the same thing by a "vivid image."
    b. provides a case in which introspection seems unproblematic because there is no worry here about sincerity, speed, or memory.
    c. is unlikely to be true because most participants have only moderately vivid images.
    d. is unproblematic because it involves an assessment of a mental product rather than a mental process.

Answer: a

18. Participants were instructed to examine four pairs of stockings and were then asked which they preferred. Participants were then asked why they had chosen the pair they had. According to the text, participants in this procedure:
    a. had no idea about why they had made their choice and could offer no response to the question.
    b. were able to respond accurately because preferences are a mental product that we can report.
    c. engaged in a process of after-the-fact reconstruction, trying to figure out why they acted as they did.
    d. felt unable to express their thought processes in words.

Answer: c

19. When asked to introspect about their reasons for making a particular choice, participants:
    a. sometimes offer an explanation with great confidence even though the explanation names factors that we know to be irrelevant, and leaves out factors that we know to be crucial.

b. can usually specify their reasons, and can also report on the processes used for selecting the reasons.

c. often have no idea about their reasons, but if they are able to report their reasons, the participants are likely to be correct.

d. can generally report their reasons in general terms but can not offer detailed accounts of their decision making.

Answer: a

20. Introspection about problem solving:
    a. helps participants to discover the key elements within the problem.
    b. seems not to influence the processes involved in problem solving.
    c. can be disruptive, making solution of the problem less likely.
    d. causes the participant to solve the problem more slowly but otherwise has no impact on the sequence of events.

Answer: c

21. In some studies, participants seem less likely to solve a problem if they have been asked to introspect about their thought processes while working on the problem. The text suggests that this effect is caused by the fact that:
    a. introspection is likely to disrupt the processes needed for successful incubation of the problem.
    b. introspection leads participants to focus on aspects of their thoughts that are easily verbalized, and these may not be the aspects crucial for solving the problem.
    c. introspection slows down the events needed for problem solving, making it more difficult to perceive the relations among those events.
    d. introspection makes participants feel self-conscious, inhibiting their ability to explore new ideas.

Answer: b

22. Freud claimed that the unconscious mind has all of the following traits except:
    a. thoughts and memories are confined to the unconscious mind because the thoughts are threatening or provoked anxiety.
    b. the unconscious mind works as a sophisticated support service, providing much of the groundwork that makes conscious thought possible.
    c. the unconscious mind is in a continual struggle with the conscious mind, with the conscious mind seeking to keep unconscious thoughts out of awareness.
    d. the unconscious mind has its own wishes and goals separate from those of the conscious mind.

Answer: b

23. The observations made by Freud:
    a. can often be explained in cognitive terms rather than in the terms Freud proposed.
    b. have turned out, like Freud's theory, to have little lasting value.
    c. remain as unexplained phenomena, obviously requiring the development of new theories.
    d. are a powerful demonstration of the truth of Freud's views.

Answer: a

24. Which of the following is not an advantage gained by relying on routine?
    a. Routine allows mental tasks to run more quickly.
    b. Routine allows one to focus attention on other aspects of a task, thus improving performance.
    c. Routine allows one to expend less effort in deciding how to execute a task.
    d. Routine allows one to consider each decision with greater care.

Answer: d

25. A reliance on routine can produce a reflex-like, uncontrollable rigidity. This sort of rigidity is visible in all of the following except:
    a. when participants proofread, they are unable to avoid inferences, so they miss the misspelled words on the page.
    b. when participants are trying to remember accurately, they are unable to avoid relying on reconstruction.
    c. even if participants hope to avoid the Stroop effect, they cannot.
    d. even though participants understand the benefits of analogy use, they seem unable to develop a strategy that will promote this use.

Answer: d

26. In many situations, a reliance on routine is either undesirable or impossible. Which of the following is *not* one of these situations?
    a. The participant is performing a task that is highly complex and that involves the coordination of many elements.
    b. The participant is performing an unfamiliar task.
    c. The participant is performing a task which, by its nature, requires frequent choices and adjustments.
    d. The participant is performing a task for which a routine is available, but the current circumstances are ones in which it would be best to avoid the habitual routine.

Answer: a

27. The fact that we are unaware of most of our mental processing is a *good* thing for all of the following reasons *except*:
    a. the processing that we are consciously aware of is sufficient to make judgments in all cases.

b. awareness of all of our processing would send us into information overload.

c. in many cases, information about our underlying mental processes would be distracting rather than helpful.

d. most tasks would be greatly slowed if we had to sort through all of the underlying processing information.

Answer: a

28. For which of the following is the lack of access to mental processes most problematic?

a. an eyewitness trying to accurately remember a crime and trying to avoid any "recollections" based on inference

b. a student reading a page of text and trying to understand the gist of what was written on the page

c. a middle-aged man tying his shoes and not trying at all to adjust or tune the steps of shoe-tying

d. an older woman working on a crossword puzzle and trying to recall the target words by any means possible

Answer: a

29. Tricia suggests to Toby that he should learn how to knit. Toby dismisses the idea, but then, several days later, announces that he has just had the wonderful idea that he should take up knitting. Research by Jacoby et al. suggests that this type of "inadvertent plagiarism":

a. cannot happen as long as we rely on well-primed pathways to decide on actions.

b. is generally blocked by conscious recollection.

c. cannot be avoided, because we all rely heavily on routine.

d. may be the result (in the present case) of Toby's repressed desire to please Tricia.

Answer: b

30. The text suggests that we are able to avoid falling into a routine and repeating ourselves endlessly because:

a. our routines are usually accompanied by feedback mechanisms that avoid repetition.

b. we don't simply rely on what is habitual or familiar; we are also able to reflect on our thoughts and on the sources of those thoughts.

c. we usually have more than one routine, appropriate for a situation, so we are able to vary performance by alternating routines.

d. our ordinary mental functioning is too complex to be accomplished by means of routine.

Answer: b

31. Blind-sight patients seem able to make many visual discriminations and, when pressed, are able to locate objects in their visual environment. Yet these same patients can not walk across a room without bumping into something. The text suggests that:
    a. blind-sight patients are able to make discriminations only when the stimuli are particularly clear.
    b. the patients can make discriminations only in controlled laboratory conditions.
    c. the patients do not feel they have a reason or justification for using the information that is apparently available to them.
    d. the patients tend to rely on routine rather than use the information that is apparently available to them.

    Answer: c

32. Participants in many experiments show clear evidence of implicit memory but fail on comparable tests of explicit memory. Yet the participants could, in principle, rely on their implicit memories to guide their guessing in the explicit test. If they did, they would perform well on the explicit tests. The text indicates that participants fail to do this because:
    a. implicit memories are memories of a sort that can not be applied to a procedure with direct memory testing.
    b. implicit memories are not detectable by the participant.
    c. participants seem to treat their implicit memories as though they were unreliable chance associations, so they do not trust them to be actual memories.
    d. participants seem to rely on implicit memories for perceptually based tasks, but not for tasks that are more conceptual in nature.

    Answer: c

33. The text argues that you will take action based on a memory:
    a. only if you are satisfied that the thought you are having is in fact an actual memory.
    b. as soon as you recall the gist of the remembered information.
    c. independent of how you assess the memory.
    d. only if the content of the memory is consistent with your other beliefs.

    Answer: a

34. The text explores the idea that the justification for action, based on some information, depends on the conscious presentation of that information. This implies all of the following claims *except*:
    a. it is the nature and quality of our conscious experience that persuades us to take information seriously.
    b. outside of laboratory circumstances, we are unlikely to be influenced by the workings of implicit memory.

    c. when our conscious experience is rich and detailed, this persuades us that the presented information is more than a fantasy or chance association.

    d. when our conscious experience is impoverished, we tend not to take action based on the information gained from that experience.

Answer: b

35. The term "qualia" refers to:

    a. the information contained within a conscious experience.

    b. the consequences of having a conscious experience.

    c. the information needed to make thought flexible and deliberate.

    d. the raw feel of an experience, reflecting how it feels to have the experience.

Answer: d

36. Which of the following clearly refers to the qualia associated with an experience?

    a. Kelsey knew where the new pizzeria was located, but she hadn't been there yet.

    b. Karen had read a lot about sky diving, but she wondered what the experience really felt like.

    c. Kate was just starting to learn about chemistry, so she did not know what color a compound would turn when she heated it.

    d. Kathy hated to go to church because it always made her think about Aunt Gertrude.

Answer: b

37. Brian selected the recipe because he knew that his guests all liked chocolate; Brian, however, did not know how the recipe would turn out. This seems to be a case in which Brian's judgment:

    a. depends on information that does not involve qualia.

    b. is influenced by qualia.

    c. requires a conscious decision, probably based on unconscious reasons.

    d. depends on consciousness.

Answer: a